NECESSARILY
BLACK

NECESSARILY BLACK

CAPE VERDEAN YOUTH, HIP-HOP CULTURE, AND A CRITIQUE OF IDENTITY

P. KHALIL SAUCIER

MICHIGAN STATE UNIVERSITY PRESS • *East Lansing*

♾ The paper used in this publication meets the minimum requirements of
ANSI/NISO Z39.48-1992 (R 1997) (Permanence of Paper).

Michigan State University Press
East Lansing, Michigan 48823-5245

Printed and bound in the United States of America.

21 20 19 18 17 16 15   1 2 3 4 5 6 7 8 9 10

Library of Congress Control Number: 2015934737
ISBN: 978-1-61186-168-6 (pbk.)
ISBN: 978-1-60917-456-9 (ebook: PDF)
ISBN: 978-1-62895-228-5 (ebook: ePub)
ISBN: 978-1-62896-228-4 (ebook: Mobi/prc)

BLACK AMERICAN AND DIASPORIC STUDIES SERIES
Curtis Stokes, *Series Editor*

Book design by Charlie Sharp, Sharp Des!gns, Lansing, Michigan
Cover design by Shaun Allshouse, www.shaunallshouse.com
Cover image is © 2014 of Khai Boa Photography and is used with
permission of artist Chachi Carvalho. All rights reserved.

Michigan State University Press is a member of the Green Press Initiative and is committed
to developing and encouraging ecologically responsible publishing practices. For more
information about the Green Press Initiative and the use of recycled paper in book
publishing, please visit *www.greenpressinitiative.org*.

Visit Michigan State University Press at *www.msupress.org*

Contents

Preface

The time approaches 10:00 P.M. and all of the black-leather booths are filled with people sipping alcoholic and nonalcoholic beverages, talking on cell phones, looking over notebooks, laughing, and texting friends. The crowd also thickens on the small dance floor at Xxodus Café at the Providence Black Repertory Company, known affectionately by regulars and locals as the Black Rep, a place that produces and presents artistic performances inspired by the cultural traditions of the African diaspora. The decor is dark and African-centered. The walls feature Dogon masks and carved wooden elephants; animal prints are carefully placed to create a chic environment. Some people are dancing in a cipher; arms are flailing, feet are kicking, and robotic motions are mimicked. Others stand with arms crossed and heads nodding. The bass line is thick and heavy, and the constant thump pounds out over the sound system, reverberating amidst the dancing and motionless bodies. Alternating between the energy-infused hip-hop performances are melodic and sublime readings of spoken word. Six days a week the scene is similar, for the Black Rep presents live music, poetry, and other live performances, contributing to the cultural literacy of the Providence community. As a result, the Black Rep is one of the more popular nightly destinations in the area. Every Monday night local hip-hop artist Charles "Chachi" Carvalho, a Cape Verdean American, hosts an open microphone, spoken word, and poetry series called "Polyphonic."

Tonight, most of the people in attendance are Cape Verdean Americans, but there are a few African Americans and white folk enjoying the music played by DJ Theron, a

Cape Verdean American. This edition of "Polyphonic" is dedicated to local Cape Verdean hip-hop artists. On a typical night the "Polyphonic" crowd is noticeably more diverse, that is, racially mixed, but tonight Cape Verdean youth are the majority. On this night, there are appearances by local Cape Verdean hip-hop artists from the Greater Boston area: DJ Lefty, Tem Blessed, Gremlin, and D. Lopes. Unlike other nights, traditional and contemporary forms of Cape Verdean music are mixed somewhat seamlessly with old school and new school hip-hop music. Wearing baggy jeans, a camouflage baseball cap, and a white T-shirt with the old flag of the Republic of Cape Verde imprinted on the front, Chachi jumps on stage and begins to kick a freestyle[1] using English, but suddenly, and to the amazement and thrill of the crowd, switches to Cape Verdean creole,[2] the national language of the Republic of Cape Verde. Similarly dressed, Tem Blessed, whose performance was no less energetic, follows Chachi. From this, it became abundantly clear that a hip-hop party, a cipher, with a Cape Verdean vibe and feeling had clearly begun. But something else was lurking, a structure of feeling that was obviously apparent, but simultaneously invisible: the specter of blackness.[3]

That was then.

Fast forward to 2013, when I was invited to deliver a public presentation on some of the material presented in this book. As I stepped to the podium and adjusted the microphone, I looked up and out toward the thirty or so individuals in attendance. My eyes were greeted by a generationally mixed crowd of Cape Verdeans from the community and a smattering of others. As I excitedly explored what my ethnographic eyes have observed over the years, I noticed that the bodily disposition (cues and postures) and facial expressions of the older Cape Verdeans, and some non–Cape Verdeans sympathetic to what I would call older Cape Verdean racial politics, began to show a tired disgust for my comments and observations on Cape Verdean blackness. Their presumed attitudinal shift, at least for me, enveloped the room. It was clear that they were tired of the seemingly infinite rehearsal of questions concerning *who* they were as a people. As time passed, the looks grew more tiresome and disgusted. The shifting in seats became more common and repetitive, many noticeably wanting to respond to my every assertion. The worn looks began to stifle my enthusiasm. I became less empathic with my observations, and in some ways I internally started second-guessing what I had concluded.

Their disapproval should have been expected given the long and complicated arc of Cape Verdean racial politics in the United States and elsewhere. As my talk concluded, we shifted to the question-and-answer period, a shift that could not have come soon enough for many in attendance (including myself, albeit for different reasons). Those most visibly annoyed were first to speak with fury about my misguided research questions, the limitations of my sample size (despite it being fairly large for an ethnographic account), the age of my participants (too young, meaning being too naïve to understand the "truth" about being Cape Verdean), and by extension my clouded conclusions. They further declared "they were more than black" that they were "human" and "should not be confined to a box," a criterion I was affirmatively told didn't exist in their home country. For many they were simply *kriolu* or Cape Verdean. "We are a cosmopolitan people," one affectionately declared. After such declarations, the elder Cape Verdeans in more robust ways fiercely circumscribed, distanced, and discredited Cape Verdean blackness.

The "we are more than black" declaration spouted with reverence more than once during the question-and-answer period did two things. First, it contradicted what I have observed Cape Verdean youth express in a variety of ways over the years, and second, it affirmed that not being black was a political maneuver and not just a factual utterance about sanguine identity. It was further evidence that nonblackness is foundational to the racial logic of the world. That in not being black (or more than black) one can begin to wage a struggle for "human" recognition, enabling one entrance into and participation in civil society. Put slightly differently, what was most disturbing about this event was how antiblack violence manifests itself in the form of ardent mixed-race identification and the vexed pronouncements of *only* and *simply* being Cape Verdean. What became clearer was that there was something about the black, in a Fanonian sense, that prompted a crisis not just in identification, but also in quality of being. Cape Verdean blackness is solely composed of the outer limit, and not the core that defines the interior of Cape Verdeanness (*caboverdianidade*). In this sense, being *kriolu* is celebrated as the antithesis of a fixed identity, especially an identity that carries with it the stigmata of nothingness. It becomes the product of an amalgamation, the product of creolization that attempts to delink blackness from Cape Verde and its diaspora.

In all this, I also noticed that the younger Cape Verdeans in attendance, those similar in age to the voices that compose this book, said or did little to be noticed. Their unassuming nature made me wonder if they too held similar sentiments, again throwing my observations into question. However, as I gathered my things with an internal disappointment, several young Cape Verdeans approached me to thank me and to agree with and confirm my observations. As one attendee stated, "They [Cape Verdean elders] needed to hear that! They need to know *what* we are in this world!" Rather than attenuating racial blackness, the youth on this day once again, as I have witnessed over the years, ethically embraced and embodied blackness.

■ ■ ■

Cape Verdean identity is complex, and over the years I have observed countless debates, many of which were emotional accounts (like the one described above), between young and old, on what it meant to *be* Cape Verdean. The variability was vast. They often debated the constitutive elements of Cape Verdeanness, which at times included one's skin color, hair texture, eye shape, and color. At other times these debates included the island's colonial past, its close proximity to the African continent, shared experiences of oppression, and its hybrid cultural features that are simultaneously European and African (and at times Chinese, Lebanese, and Jewish) among many other things. Cape Verdean identity, no doubt, complicates essentialized observations about racial identity, for the Cape Verdean diaspora is a highly nuanced and complicated entity composed of and concealing a variety of positions and communities, but to write about Cape Verdean blackness does not uncomplicate these matters. Rather, it gestures to the ways in which racial identity on the one hand can be fluid and contextual, but race as more than identity—as a structural position—is not. The reality is that Cape Verdean youth often find themselves confronted by a racial system in the United States that configures them as black within the narrow cultural logic of its binary black/nonblack racial structure. Under these conditions, and for these youth, to be simply Cape Verdean is a vexed position and, as many of them elaborated, frankly dishonest.

Necessarily Black: Cape Verdean Youth, Hip-Hop Culture, and a Critique of Identity is about the variety of ways Cape Verdean youth in the northeast embody blackness in terms of both comportment and meaning, but also including the disciplinary practices to which black bodies are subject. The cultural practices, namely hip-hop cultural practices, explored in this book simultaneously complicate, challenge, and affirm certain beliefs about race and racial identity. What becomes apparent in *Necessarily Black* is that blackness is a position that is also distinct from an identity. This means *Necessarily Black* understands "Blackness not [only]—in the first instance—as a variously and unconsciously interpellated identity or as a conscious social actor, but as a structural position of non-communicability in the face of all other positions" (Wilderson 2010, 58). Cape Verdean youth help make this rather rich abstraction real, as exhibited in their lived experiences that make up these pages.

The approach developed in *Necessarily Black* posits that we, as scholars and laypeople, have a good deal more to learn about race and more specifically the centrality of blackness in everyday life. And in doing so we should strive not to reproduce the very antiblack structures that are *the* problem, although not the only problem, in the first place. This ethnography, while attentive to the present and the minutiae of everyday life, is ultimately anchored in the past. That is, as Huey Copeland limns in *Bound to Appear*, "to think in such structural terms [as *Necessarily Black* does] is not to essentialize what are historically contingent practices and identities, but to position them in relationship to a centuries-old antiglobal hierarchy, which darkens the marginal, the fugitive, and the socially dead wherever they appear" (2013, 11). *Necessarily Black* attempts to apprehend via the Cape Verdean subject what "it means to be an embodied subject now . . . caught up in economies of race, affect, and reification whose coordinates remain as much real as imaginary" (22).

Necessarily Black illustrates that ethnic and cultural variability do little to mitigate the social fact that being racialized as black and being black in the world is still a mortal challenge. With the wholesale adoption of the multicultural paradigm and color-blind rhetoric from the state and civil society, critical attention has been deflected from an increasingly antiblack world. The recourse to color-blind rhetoric and its commitments of inclusion, hybridity, and diversity omit historical memory and material relations of power, the lineaments of antiblackness. During the post–civil rights period, we have witnessed the repressive silencing of the ongoing and determinant role race, and more specifically antiblackness, plays in global life, that is, its importance in power relations, resources, affect, land, and labor. As Africana philosopher Lewis Gordon writes in *Disciplinary Decadence*, "particularly egregious is the continued tendency, or perhaps willful effort to misrepresent the realities of black folk" (2007, 30). Our understanding of race and processes of racialization are incomplete, making living in an antiblack world all the more difficult. While ideas are easy to throw out the proverbial window, the embodiment of these concepts in lived experiences cannot be dismissed so readily. Blackness is continuously being externally and internally produced and reproduced in the real world, thus giving it conceptual meaning and social life. White supremacy and antiblackness are paradigmatic, and as a result race still matters, for it still structures existence (see Jung, Vargas, and Bonilla-Silva 2011). White supremacy and antiblackness hold sway in the political, judicial, cultural, cognitive, economic, somatic, and metaphysical spheres of society (see Mills 1998, 2013). And given that race is historical and contextual (Du Bois 1897), thus constantly changing, yet obdurate, our understanding of race and processes of racialization is never more in need if we are to move beyond this world.

America is decidedly not postracial or color-blind. One need only observe the murder of Trayvon Martin or Oscar Grant, the drug war, the debate around affirmative racial policies, the hyperincarceration of black people, the response to the atrocities of Hurricane Katrina, stop-and-frisk policies, or the countless other murderous and gratuitous activities that go unrevealed to know that blackness, despite all its nuance and variability, still matters. The desire to move beyond race, which is to say blackness, is evidence that society is not only unwilling to openly face its past, a past filled with deception and death, but also unwilling to face the fact that race and more specifically antiblackness is at the vortex of everyday life, it is that which haunts the banality of life, that which creates what Christina Sharpe (2010) has called "monstrous intimacies." If we fail to examine race, processes of racialization, and racial identity in the twenty-first century, we fail to understand how many, in this case Cape Verdean youth, are reacting to the paradigm and its attendant practices and how those things are (re)constituting black identities and ontologies. To this end, in order to produce an antiracist politics (or an antepolitics) that is successful and forward thinking, and dare I say revolutionary, we must understand the contemporary terrain of race and racial meaning, thus to recognize the centrality of antiblackness. Theories about race must be self-reflexive, that is, they must always reexamine and refine the ways in which they explore race, racism(s), and racial identity. In a few words, they must be ruthlessly critical of all existing theories. Given that both my theoretical and methodological orientation are informed by black studies and critical theory, I, like most critical researchers, assume that the knowledge developed in these pages may serve as an additional step toward addressing injustices associated with blackness. In other words, I am not simply interested in knowledge for knowledge's sake, but rather in producing a critical intervention that allows us to more fully comprehend blackness on a global scale. *Necessarily Black* is my attempt to adhere to Du Bois's call for a more humanistic and authentic account of black life; a more realistic account of what Jared Sexton has called "the social life of social death" (2011). And hopefully, *Necessarily Black* will help contribute to the idea that blackness as embodied and embraced by Cape Verdean youth is also where life is reinvented.

Acknowledgments

Necessarily Black would have not been possible without the assistance, inspiration, and fellowship of colleagues, comrades, and friends, both far and wide. I would like to thank Mike Brown for his amazing insight, support, generosity, and encouragement. It is difficult to imagine what would have come of this project, and me, were it not for his intellectual brilliance and sophistication. My earnest appreciation goes to Tryon Woods for always asking more of me. His insight and constructive criticism over the past couple of years has made me a better scholar. I am grateful for his unwavering encouragement to keep writing. Abundant thanks to Murray Forman for his generosity, friendship, critical dialogue, and commitment since I started developing this project. I am also grateful to Christina Sharpe for her friendship and goodwill. Sincere thanks to George Yancy, Joy James, Lewis R. Gordon, James Manigault-Bryant, Rhon Manigault-Bryant, Frank Wilderson III, Sabine Broeck, Wini Breines, Tamara Nopper, Roderick Graham, Matt Hunt, Kumirini Silva, Richard Lobban, Reiland Rabaka, and many others. Thank you also to the insightful scholars who have written and who will write on all things necessary for a better world.

My deepest gratitude goes to Curtis Stokes, Series Editor at Michigan State University Press, for his support and enthusiasm for this project. I would also like to thank Editor in Chief Julie Loehr and Elise Jajuga for their guidance in this whole process. Thanks to the anonymous manuscript reviewers for their careful responses and important intellectual interventions.

Some of the material in this book appears with the kind permission of the publishers. An earlier version of chapter 2 appeared as "Becoming Black? Race and Racial Identity among Cape Verdean Youth," in the collection *Migrant Marginality: A Transnational Perspective* (New York: Routledge, 2014) edited by Philip Kretsedemas, Jorge Capetillo-Ponce, and Glenn Jacobs. It has been reproduced with the permission of Taylor and Francis Group. Chapter 4 appeared in a slightly revised form as "Cape Verdean Youth Fashion: Identity in Clothing," in *Fashion Theory* 15, no. 1 (March 2011); reprinted with permission. And chapter 5 appeared in a different version as "CVSpace: Musings on Cape Verdean Identity, Technology, and MySpace," in *The American Communication Journal* 11, no. 1 (Spring 2009); reprinted with permission.

I would also like to thank all the Cape Verdean youth throughout the Greater Boston area that took the time to sit with me and answer my questions. Although not everyone made it into the manuscript, all your comments, suggestions, and insights on race, identity, and popular culture in the United States left an indelible mark in the following pages. Muito obrigado!

And to the most beautiful person I have ever met in my life, my wife and partner, Jasmine. Thank you for your intense love and example.

Introduction

I provide in *Necessarily Black* an ethnographic account of second-generation Cape Verdean youth identity in the Greater Boston area and a theoretical attempt to broaden and complicate current discussions around race and racial identity (subjectivities) in the twenty-first century. In the last five decades the United States has experienced large-scale immigration particularly from Asia, Latin America, and Africa. Africans, especially from sub-Saharan Africa, represent one of the fastest-growing segments of the United States' immigrant population. Today, there are millions of African immigrants and their children in the United States. Without a doubt, the cultural polyphony of Africans has become a noticeable aspect particularly of the urban landscape of major metropolitan centers across the United States, and for many it is thought to be transforming the character of race relations and racial and ethnic categories.[1] In *Problematizing Blackness*, for instance, Percy Hintzen and Jean Muteba Rahier state, "black immigrants, by their growing presence, are contributing to the unsettling and destabilizing of the meaning of blackness in the United States and to the process, almost organic, of its deconstruction" (2003, 2). As the number of African immigrants has expanded, their children have gradually entered mainstream institutions like secondary and postsecondary schools, community centers, and the workplace, and as a result have increasingly become more visible. Despite the plurality of black identities, African immigrants and their children often find they are confronted by a racial system, which is simultaneously global and local, that configures them one-dimensionally and structurally as black.[2]

Cape Verdean immigrants are no exception, for the Cape Verdean diaspora in the Greater Boston area has consistently grown since the 1960s. As Marilyn Halter (1993), Gina Sánchez Gibau (1997, 2005), and more recently Ambrizeth Lima (2011) have argued, the Cape Verdean diaspora has actively contested the boundaries of racial categories in the United States by creating a space for cultural differentiation. However, these studies use the narratives of Cape Verdeans only and have failed to investigate the "sites through which racial meanings are crafted" (Pierre 2013, 2), areas such as popular culture. Both Sánchez Gibau (1997, 2005) and Lima (2011) only briefly allude to the import of popular culture and Cape Verdean youth. Further, many of these early studies (Halter 1993; Meintel 1981; Sánchez Gibau 1997, 2005) focus only on first-generation Cape Verdeans. It is reasonable to assume, especially given the wave of Cape Verdean community in the United States, that many Cape Verdean youth have come of age living with other racial and ethnic minorities and are producers and consumers of black popular culture. As a result, the processes of racialization (or more specifically the process of blackening) that Cape Verdean youth confront and adhere to, and sometimes disrupt, are fundamentally much different from their parents' generation, a fact that points toward the vacuity of contemporary discourse on Cape Verdean subjectivities in the United States. The problem with most, if not all, studies on Cape Verdeanness is that they are not fully accountable to blackness.

In general, identity is experienced, performed, communicated, and engaged in various sociocultural practices. Racial subjectivities, whether diasporic, transnational, or not, are no different. They are constructed out of a process of negotiation and contestation, but the negotiation and contestation are delimited by a structure of racial logic that positions blacks outside the global human family, which is to say outside the discursive and material formations of *the human*. Although these notions of who is human are the product of Western culture, through the global reach of Western imperialism (colonialism and racial slavery) these ideas have achieved a degree of worldwide hegemony (see Barrett 2014; Bogues 2012; Da Silva 2007; Thomas 2007; Wynter 2003).

I attempt to understand Cape Verdean identity within this global structure of racial blackness. I am concerned to elucidate the ways in which discursive acts and ideological practices give race social significance as well as the cultural and political ways that blackness is invoked to give meaning to social and cultural phenomena. To this end, I grapple with the performance, embodiment, and nuances of racialized identities (blackened bodies) in empirical contexts. I look into the durability and (in)flexibility of race and racial discourse through an imbricated and multidimensional understanding of racial identity and racial positioning. In doing so, I examine how second-generation Cape Verdean youth in the Greater Boston area negotiate their identity within the popular fabrication of "multiracial America." I explore they ways in which racial blackness has come to be *lived* by Cape Verdean youth in everyday life and, accordingly, how racialization feeds back into the lived experience of these youth classified as black through a matrix of social and material settings. However, I am not satisfied with simply exploring the assignation and appropriation of blackness; rather, I am interested above all about how the youth embody racial blackness: how do they live out the way in which global structures and local histories of racial blackness assemble themselves on their very bodies and in the intimate spaces of their communities? This is to say, I attend to the phenomenology of Cape Verdean racial embodiment, not the nuance of racial identity. In other words, what ontology is implied by the persistence of blackness that haunts the Cape Verdean body and lived experience? Rather than figuring Cape Verdean identity as mere effect of racialized subjection, I look at the ways in which Cape Verdean blackness is reframed through the recourse of everyday life.

I examine how ascriptions of blackness and forms of black popular culture inform subjectivities. More specifically, I examine hip-hop culture to see how it is used as a site where new (and/or old) identities of being, becoming, and belonging are fashioned and reworked within the contemporary sociocultural context of race in the early twenty-first century. Hip-hop culture is understood to be one of many "racial projects" that help constitute the building blocks of racialization. My approach is not to speak for the totality and entirety of the Cape Verdean lived experience; rather it is to focus on some of the racial projects that were important to my informants and to those that work to continue to give race meaning (or force) and by extension contribute to our understanding of black positionality. I am not arguing that all Cape Verdean youth are the same, especially in reference to ethnicity, national belonging, and class. I do not deny or diminish the significance of these modalities of being. Instead, my overall trajectory is that blackness is the modality through which many of these identifications continue to be structured.

In pursuit of these ends, I also attend to another agenda, one that subtends the matter of racial analytics but also extends it: the sociohistorical problematic of sociology itself. Along with the other social sciences, the sociology discipline has thought black racial identity in certain theoretically and politically treacherous ways—including, most overwhelmingly, finding a litany of modes in which to *not* think of it at all (Hartman and Wilderson 2003). Here I attempt to provide an ethnography of embodiment, while attempting to theorize blackness among Cape Verdean youth in the twenty-first century. I focus on the mysterious workings of race and how Cape Verdean youth *think* and *feel* their identities into palpable everyday existence, while keeping in mind the dynamics and politics of racialization, mixed-race identities, and antiblackness.

FADE TO ANTIBLACKNESS

Because race is typically understood solely as an ideology, a discourse, or a discursive act, it often gets translated as a merely cultural representation and performance of certain people, and not as the people themselves.[3] Since racial identities are thought to be neither biologically determined nor socially stable they rely on an ongoing process of performance. Racial identity is achieved or not achieved based on one's actions and how others interpret them. According to this insight, race is something one does, an act, or more precisely, a sequence of acts that *accomplish* a racial identity. Race is performed through phenotype, skin color, and a range of cultural signifiers such as music, language, and clothing.[4] These qualities act together and communicate racial subjectivity. While racial identity is considered to be unstable, certain racial performances have become normative, produced out of the discourse that it names. Again, it is thought that race is culturally and socially configured, while falsely naturalized through reification, in order to uphold forms of cultural hegemony. For example, racial identity through the use of hip-hop culture serves to reify certain reductive ideas and ways of being black in the world, that is, ways of presenting one's self as black given a specific audience. Further, and more importantly, the discourse of hip-hop signals for race, in this case blackness, to be performed in a certain way. What is required for this shared sense of blackness, then, is a continual repetition of blackness in the everyday; race is accumulated through the repetition of discourse. The embodiment of hip-hop culture, to be hip-hop, makes the materiality of the Cape Verdean black body solidify. Hip-hop culture becomes central, for that is what is important. On the one hand, hip-hop helps condition and create blacks. On the other hand, it allows entry and access; it enables membership. Put differently, hip-hop culture is a force of orientation. Hip-hop style (of conduct) and fashion fits with the bodily schema. Habits of bodily organization and/or conduct, that is to say embodiment, enable our perception of Cape Verdean youth as black. Cape Verdean youth are habituated into disposing their bodies in ways unique to their situation *as* black.

Although I engage with popular culture and therefore understand race as discursive and ideological, I do so from the understanding that the discursive and ideological are only part of the investigatory equation attempted within these pages. Race therefore is also approached and understood to be ontological. In this sense, race has as much to do with the body as it does cultural representations. It is a set of sociopolitical processes underwritten by the materiality of the body, something Alex Weheliye (2014) calls racializing assemblages (see also Saldanha 2006, 2010). The phenotypic black body, as we will see, goes beyond ethnic and cultural difference. The "fact of blackness" is the understanding that race is a social dimension, a categorical distortion encoded on the skin (Fanon 1967; Raengo 2013; Wiegman 1995).The mark that accompanies blackness is not reversible. Antiblackness is a social fact that materializes into black (abject) flesh (Spillers 2003). As Peter Wolfe has stated, "race is not a negotiable condition but a destiny, one whose outward sign is the body" (2002, 52). In this sense, therefore, race is a material process in that it is based on how different types of people interact, partake in social action, and gradually become divided and categorized into racial groups. Despite the import of the body, I am not endorsing a mute physicality. The body, I am simply arguing, becomes an evidential marker of difference that is then connected to forms of social action. To this end, the raced body needs to be understood as a vessel for experience, what Hook (2008) calls "expressive phenomenology." The body is simultaneously ideological and a space of affectivity. Seeing the body as a vessel for affectivity allows us to assume that resistance is possible, that the ideological body is never totally performed or subsumed by the discursive. In this sense, race is contingent and necessary, it cannot be transcended in this world, and it can only be discursively and performatively rearranged. In other words, race as a historical structure laid over specific bodies both shapes the meaning of these bodies in action and delimits their capacity to transcend the world's structuring logic.

This book is slightly different from other ethnographies on blackness, for antiblackness is a primary focus and not white supremacy.[5] More often than not, ethnographies on blackness seek solely to challenge discursive and ideological understandings of blackness, and in return, racism is not in the foreground but in the background; it is the backdrop for descriptive accounts of black variability through time and space. Many ethnographies on race fail to go beyond identity and therefore do not map the relations of power that existed in the past and those that exist today. The problem with a great deal of racial studies scholarship, critical or otherwise, is that they fail to take stock in what is constitutive of *all* black identities and subjectivities. Black identity (as an illustration of agency) must always be prefigured by the concept of blackness. The overarching failures of these works are that they are too interested in agency at the expense of ontology, that is, the ways in which ontological limitations created by the structures of antiblackness already delimit agency. In other words, they are not always attentive to the processes of antiblackness that mark every scale of black subjectivity in everyday life.

While I do complicate blackness as identity, I also deal with the limitations of such nuance as well as the obdurate, steadfast, diabolical, and global persistence of anti-blackness that structurally positions people outside human relations. It is de rigueur to define racial identity as fluid, constructed, and unstable. In doing so, racial identity politics often rest on a mistaken view of the subject that is ontologically prior to any form of oppression and/or death. Let me be clear, I am not disregarding identity, simply relocating it.[6] Bringing together ontological questions and ethnographic observation about the deployment, practice, and embodiment of racial identity is not a farfetched idea, for being seen as nothing, as less-than-human, which is to say black, generates the question "who am I?" that in turn generates the question "what am I?" In studies on race, and more so racial identity, the "who" is the only question that gets answered, as if answering the "what" essentializes the person's identity in practice. This is based on the same logic that to talk about racism is to practice racism. The connection between identity and ontology is fabulously detailed by philosopher Mabogo More when he states, "Since questions of identity naturally imply beings' relation to itself, they ultimately become ontological questions of being, essence, and meaning which then take the form of 'What am I?'" (2012, 26). With certainty, questions about identity immediately throw us into the realm of ontology.

In defining race, it is easy to be seduced by the blanket statement that it is simply a social construction.[7] Take for instance Michael Omi and Howard Winant's frequently cited definition of race. They argue that "race is a concept which signifies and symbolizes social conflicts and interests by referring to different types of human bodies." They go on to state that race is "an unstable and 'decentered' complex of social meanings constantly being transformed by political struggle" (1994, 55). In conceptualizing race in this fashion, racial difference is understood to be prepolitical rather than the result of Western modernity. Race is understood to presuppose (although not in a biological sense, thus eliminating a naturalized view of race) the social and does not account for the ways in which race is constituted as both an epistemological and ontological category. This is to say that race, and by extension blackness, is a modern category and therefore has ontological status and import. In line with such thinking is David Theo Goldberg's account that "race is imposed upon otherness, the attempt to account for it, to know it, to control it. . . . But paradoxically, once racially configured with modernity the threat becomes magnified, especially fraught, because in being named racially in a sense that it is named as threat. . . . The racial conception of the state [and civil society] becomes the racial definition of the apparatus, the project, the institutions for managing this threat, for keeping it out or ultimately containing it—but also (and gains paradoxically) for keeping it" (2002, 23–24). Or more simply, as Sylvia Wynter has argued, "the damned of the earth" were forced into "the matrix slot of otherness—made into the physical referent of the idea of irrational/subrational Human other" (2003, 261). Each of these observations, unlike Omi and Winant, gesture to the ontological constitution of race, which is why ontology must, at the very least, have a passing presence in any discussion or investigation into race as a category and concept, lived or otherwise. In this sense, racialization is always the reflection of the modern knowledge apparatus whether accomplished by the state or by civil society.

Since antiblackness defines the scope and quality of human *beings*, it asks who and what qualifies as human. In doing so, it locates, marks, and positions those who will be disposable, those who will know gratuitous violence (Wilderson 2010), those who were never meant to survive (Vargas 2008). As Mabogo More argues, "in human terms, to live under the threat of non-being is to live in what existentialists call a condition of finitude, the constant possibility of disintegration and death and, therefore, anguish and anxiety" (2012, 31). Being black in an antiblack world is to be rendered a nonbeing and to create doubt concerning the humanity of the black, a doubt that has the potential to extend to self-understanding (Gordon 1995a, 2000).[8]

In short, antiblackness is a symbolic order that marks and values human lives in relation to nonblackness; white supremacy is therefore not the scaffolding from which, at least in this case, Cape Verdean subjectivities are negotiated and articulated. This is to say that antiblackness and white supremacy are not the same thing. Far too often antiblackness is either subsumed under white supremacy as antiblack racism only or simply conflated as white supremacy (see Smith 2010). As the historical register makes clear, antiblackness precedes the emergence of white supremacy (Farley 1997; Robinson 2000; Wilderson 2010). The scales of violence that are calibrated along those who are and those who are not human is globally constant despite the complexity of transnational flows and diversity of nation-states (Woods 2007). Since antiblackness is a symbolic order that affects modes of being (ontology) and knowing (epistemology) it inevitably haunts our understanding of racial subjectivities, whether in social scientific literature or everyday life. I believe, then, to attend to the singularity of antiblackness "teaches us all how we might better inhabit multiplicity under general conditions at the global scale" (Sexton 2011, 8).

Being attentive to the specificity and particularity of antiblackness in the world allows us to centralize blackness, as many of my informants have done, as the base for establishing conditions of possibility (Vargas and James 2012). Antiblackness in this regard was not presupposed but an outcome of meeting my informants where they were in the world. It informs and shapes the everyday settings where Cape Verdean youth negotiate and confront the significance of blackness in the world. For more precision, Frantz Fanon's insight in *Black Skin, White Mask* (1967) is instructive. For Fanon, the construction of himself is the coming together of his body, as imagined by the world. Cape Verdean youth are forced to take up the imposed history that Fanon explicates, known as the historical racial schema as well as the racial epidermal schema. As a result, the black subject does exist, but only within the confines of this world, an antiblack world. As I hope to make apparent, Cape Verdean blackness is always subject to the imposition of both the epidermal racial schema and the historical racial schema, and as a result Cape Verdean youth are living in the libidinal and temporal shadows of antiblackness. Black skin is the metonymic sign of this mythology. For Fanon, then, racialization is the process by which difference among Africans and black people are conflated under the label Negro. With this in mind, a contrapuntal reading of the lived experience of Cape Verdean blackness and the fact of Cape Verdean blackness (ontology) is needed. Racial identity and processes of racialization are variable and explanatory, whereas ontology seeks a classification that is consistent with others classified as black; ontology provides directionality: one's racialized body ostensibly governs what one does or is able to do in the world.

Given the richness of my informants' insights, I am convinced that appeals to "the black experience," "the black world," and "African diaspora" are not essential monikers, but markers for the structural position of being black in an antiblack world (Gordon 2000; More 2012). As Katerina Deliovsky and Tamari Kitossa argue, "the significance of anti-blackness must be apprehended, not as a superior form of oppression but as a form that gives shape and context to the oppression of other racially marginalized people" (2013, 173). In short, antiblackness underlies Cape Verdean identity politics and politics of identification (Vargas 2006). Antiblackness creates and reproduces the recursive and oppressively limiting epistemologies of the Cape Verdean subject.

Processes of racialization are reflected in the title of this book by the prominence of the adverb *necessarily*, an adverb of logical consequence.[9] This speaks to the ways in which one is blackened, or made racial, first by being the repository of racism, of gratuitous violence. Not the reverse. What follows then is that Cape Verdean youth react to such acts and actions that then have a common effect, the effect of blackening. The point here is that race has its origin in acts of violence perpetrated on certain bodies, but it is also the result of actions performed and embodied at various times and in different contexts by people, in this case Cape Verdean youth. Seen from this perspective, Cape Verdean youth are structurally positioned as black, which provides them with particular (non)relations, and hence certain cultural forms and built environments, which are then the result of the creative play of these influences and things. In other words, Cape Verdean blackness is also contingent on opportunity, and action and performance are produced out of confluences of opportunities. Their structural position puts them in reach of some things (i.e., bodies, spaces, and objects) to which they must respond and react.

In the Field

Necessarily Black is the culmination of fieldwork conducted in the Greater Boston area over the course of many years. As was necessary, it entailed informal and formal interviewing, participant observation, and textual analysis. While no single methodology is superior, this project borrowed most from critical ethnography—that is, a perspective through which the researcher can frame questions and promote social action (Madison 2005). This ethnography is less about signs of Cape Verdean blackness and more about the ways in which ethnography can become a way in which social theory is produced. That is, a way to develop languages of the racial that help us to make better sense of the world in which we live so that we may respond accordingly and not simply react.

Although I have been engaged with the Cape Verdean community in the Greater Boston area for the better part of two decades, formal interest in mapping the funk and vivacity of Cape Verdean blackness commenced in 2007. My criteria in selecting participants/informants were that they had to be between the ages of eighteen and twenty-five, to be from the Greater Boston area, and to identify as second-generation Cape Verdeans or Cape Verdean Americans. The term "second generation" refers both to the American-born youth of Cape Verdean parents and to Cape Verdean–born youth who came to the United States prior to age eight. The literature on immigrant youth who straddle this line are often referred to as the 1.5 generation, a label I find cumbersome. Further, I include this group because they have spent the majority of their young existence in the United States and are culturally similar, based on previous contact, interpretation, and initial fieldwork preparation, to American-born Cape Verdean youth. Also important to mapping Cape Verdean youth identity was identifying public Cape Verdean–orientated cultural events. In my search, I identified and attended several annual, biannual, and weekly cultural events that were directed toward Cape Verdeans in general, and Cape Verdean youth more specifically. These events included, but were not limited to, the annual Independence Day festivals of the cities of Brockton, New Bedford, and Providence; college and university student gatherings and celebrations; and local hip-hop gatherings and shows. While some events were more inclusive of all types of people and backgrounds, they all shared a common relationship with Cape Verdean people in diaspora.

I chose to conduct my fieldwork in the Greater Boston area for two reasons. The first reason was my embeddedness in and familiarity with the Cape Verdean community in the area. Over the years I have created and sustained relationships with teachers, administrators, community center directors, community leaders, and others. Second, the area, which includes Boston and other surrounding urban areas such as Brockton, Cambridge, Fall River, New Bedford, Providence, Rhode Island, and Pawtucket, Rhode Island, is home to a large and established Cape Verdean diasporic community. Given the size of the Cape Verdean population in this area, the Greater Boston area is a fascinating site for investigating how local understandings and performances of race and racial identities articulate with larger processes of racialization.

While I hope to explain and describe Cape Verdean youth blackness, I do not provide causal or definitive accounts of Cape Verdean youth identity or racial and ethnic identity as a whole. Rather what is to come in the following pages is a partial description, a rehearsal of sorts, and provisional explanation of Cape Verdean youth blackness. Thus, *Necessarily Black* is more suggestive than it is definitive. In short, what follows is my attempt at entering into the dialogue on the assemblages of race, ethnicity, and popular culture in order to give a more comprehensive grasp of the racial matters (that dark matter) in question.

Making Sense of Light-Skin African Blood:
The Grammar of Cape Verdean Identity

If I'm not black, then what am I? . . . Once you have a mix in you, you're black.

—Informant

One trip to the Republic of Cape Verde, one look at its people and their phenotypic and pigmentary variation, and one becomes acutely aware of the generations of extensive intercontinental admixture. In 2010, Jorge Rocha, professor of molecular pathology and immunology at the University of Porto (Portugal), presented evidence from his study entitled "Genetic Diversity in Cape Verde." Rocha argued that "the Cape Verdean population is one of the most mixed in the world," with nearly 60 percent of genes coming from Africa and 40 percent from Europe. He praised the islands for their biodiversity, which, at times, is more diverse than Brazil. Rocha's study, which evaluated the miscegenation levels of each island through an accounting of eye color, pigmentation (i.e., using a melanin index), and other genetic markers, was meticulous and scientifically thorough. The island of Santiago is the most African, according to Rocha (2010), with Fogo showing the highest levels of miscegenation. The point of the study was not only to illustrate the extraordinary biodiversity of the islands, but also an attempt to locate the genes that produce skin color and eye color. While I am not suggesting Rocha and others have malicious intentions, such studies do remind me of Fanon's satirical prose on scientists in laboratories in search of a "denigrification serum" for "Negroes to whiten themselves and thus throw off the burden of that 'corporeal malediction'" (Fanon 1967, 111). Ironically, living in "postracial" times has meant the proliferation of genetic testing and other forms of "racial scientific" exploration. What I think is interesting about this science, which really only confirms what we already know, is that it does little to sublate or reduce the materiality of the black Cape Verdean position. Knowing that Cape Verdeans are genetically mixed does not make mixed-race identity any more real or race as structural position any less so.

In *The Amalgamation Waltz: Race, Performance, and the Ruse of Memory*, Tavia Nyong'o argues that "racial mixing and hybridity are neither problems for, nor solutions to, the long history of 'race' and racism, but parts of its genealogy" (2009, 174). Therefore this chapter offers a partial accounting of the history and grammar of Cape Verdean identity politics so as to provide the context from which Cape Verdean blackness is enunciated (Wilderson 2009). What becomes clear in looking into the history of Cape Verde and the making of its diaspora are the ways in which miscegenation and amalgamation are fashionably presented in the discourse concerning Cape Verdean subjectivities. That is, Cape Verdean subjectivities are presented with little indica- tion of the ways race rules performatively or the "schemes" that they simultaneously underwrite (see Ehlers 2012; Sexton 2010). In other words, much of what has been said about Cape Verdean identity, both historically and sociologically, implicitly and at times explicitly revolves around ways of not *being* black; there are persistent attempts to explain away manifest blackness. Rhett Jones in his important, yet seldom utilized essay "Mulattos, Freejacks, Cape Verdeans, Black Seminoles, and Others: Afrocentri- cism and Mixed-Race Persons" argues with particular reference to Cape Verdeans:

> So while the mixed-race people were not convinced they were not white or In- dian, they were convinced they were not black. A perspective . . . [that] enabled them to construct a worldview which did not see their Africanity. This was no small achievement. Not one of these communities was so backward that it did not have mirrors so that each day these people could see their despised African physical features reflected back at them. Yet they managed to together construct communities of denial in which, despite the mark of oppression, they were not black. (Jones 2003, 282)

Another problem with the discourse surrounding Cape Verdean identity is that many Cape Verdean youth do not experience the world as mixed race, but as an antagonistic element of society.[1] This complicates the question, what does it mean to be mixed race? Or more specifically, for our purposes, what does it mean to be *kriolu*? In locating some of the problems within mixed race studies, and with this I include previous scholarship on Cape Verdean identity, we are able to explore efforts of racial transcendence alongside the entrenchment and the infinite rehearsal of antiblackness. While Cape Verdean identity has not been a constitutive object of study within mixed race studies, critical or otherwise, the conceptual analytics of mixed race studies, it would seem, better facilitate a more robust understanding of Cape Verdean subjectivity. This focus is motivated by my hesitation for all "mixed" race identities to be subsumed under certain fields of study that upon closer analysis are replete with categorical errors.[2] As a result, after discussion of Cape Verdean migration, race and cultural identity, and mixed-race theory, I offer a brief note on the black/nonblack binary and a triangulated approach to better understanding Cape Verdean youth blackness.

CAPE VERDEAN MIGRATION AND THE MAKING OF DIASPORA

As Colm Foy (1988) has described, there have been two ways to escape the drought-scourged reality of the Cape Verde Islands, death or emigration.[3] In *The Fortunate Islands* (1990), Basil Davidson adds that on top of environmental forces, the Portuguese established a "system of ruin" in order to force the island residents to leave. Thus the history of Cape Verde has been shaped tremendously by emigration. Today, the motivation to leave Cape Verde is connected to the inhospitable landscape, which is made all the more difficult by poverty and high levels of unemployment (see Batalha and Carling 2008; Carling 2002; Fikes 2009; Lobban and Saucier 2007). The Cape Verdean diaspora is transnational in that there is a constant flow of people, culture, and capital to and from the islands; in many ways Cape Verdean nationalism is diasporic, rather than the reverse.[4] Similar to many former colonies, Cape Verde also allows those in the diaspora to maintain dual citizenship. The diaspora, as a result, has developed long-term cultural connections with the archipelago. The transnationalism of Cape Verdeans has led to what some call the emergence of a bilateral diaspora ethnicity (Pires-Hester 1994).

In the second half of the nineteenth century, many Cape Verdeans, mainly from Brava and Fogo, immigrated to the United States to seek work in the whaling industry and packet trade. This laid the foundation for a substantial immigration to the United States at the turn of the twentieth century. Roughly 1,500 Cape Verdean migrants arrived annually on packet ships between 1860 and 1920; during those years, 26,585 Cape Verdean immigrants arrived in New England (Coli and Lobban 1990, 5–7).

They settled mainly in New Bedford, Massachusetts. With the decline of the whaling industry and packet trade, many went to work in agriculture—picking strawberries and cranberries—and in factories, settling in Massachusetts (New Bedford, Boston, Plymouth, Taunton, Brockton, Cape Cod), Rhode Island (Pawtucket, East Providence, Central Falls), Connecticut, New York, Florida, Hawaii, and California. Nearly one-third of all Cape Verdeans arriving in the New England area between 1900 and 1920 listed Plymouth County as their intended destination (Lobban and Saucier 2007, 68). The introduction of immigration quotas in the 1920s—the Immigration Acts of 1921 and 1924—derailed Cape Verdean immigration to the United States for nearly five decades. In the 1960s and early 1970s, with the demand for workers in Europe and strict immigration limitations in the United States, as outlined in the Immigration and Nationality Act of 1965, many Cape Verdeans chose to immigrate to Europe, particularly to Portugal and the Netherlands. However, even with independence in 1975, the flow of immigrants continued. Today, there exists a strong migratory flow to Portugal, Brazil, the Netherlands, Italy, France, Luxemburg, Sweden, and Germany. Others have immigrated to Angola, Senegal, and Argentina. Of all the destinations, Portugal, the Netherlands, France, and the United States are most important.

The number of Cape Verdeans in the diaspora probably outnumbers the population of the republic. However, quantifying the Cape Verdean diaspora is difficult. The reliability and validity of the data is also questionable. The Cape Verdean government, for instance, tracks people entering and exiting the country from all ports and airports, but the type of journey one is embarking on is never specified. As Jorgen Carling (2002) has pointed out, quantifying diasporic populations is tricky because of overlapping categories of citizenship, nativity, ethnicity, and issues of mobility. Problems with quantifying the Cape Verdean diaspora population include the number of undocumented Cape Verdeans, those who emigrated when Cape Verdeans held Portuguese passports, those of mixed "ancestry," and the increasing number of third- and fourth-generation Cape Verdeans. The latter are common especially in the Greater Boston area. Nonetheless, the best estimate puts the Cape Verdean diaspora around 700,000 people (IOM 2010).

One of the oldest and largest Cape Verdean diasporic populations lives in the United States, particularly in the Greater Boston area. Many of its members come from the islands of Fogo and Brava, followed by Sal and Sao Vincente. In 2000, the U.S. Census reported less than 80,000 Cape Verdeans in the United States.[5] Others have estimated that the number is closer to 300,000 or more. The Greater Boston area alone is estimated to have 255,000 Cape Verdeans (Instituto das Comunidades 2007).

RACE AND CULTURAL IDENTITY IN CAPE VERDE AND IN DIASPORA

Due to its important position within the transatlantic slave trade, Cape Verde served as a meeting place for various peoples. As a result, a *kriolu* or *mestiço* population emerged in the islands. In a very basic sense, Cape Verdean people are decedents of Portuguese and African people. During the initial phase of colonization and subjection there existed only two racial groups in Cape Verde: *brancos*, "whites," and *prêtos*, "blacks." The *brancos* consisted of upper-class noblemen and merchants, while *prêtos* were more often than not slaves. During the early days of Portuguese colonization, *prêtos* were the overwhelming majority of the bipolar system. However this system, according to anthropologist Richard Lobban, vanished within a few short years for "it was common practice for slave masters to have sexual relations with their slaves, especially when so many Portuguese masters did not bring their wives into their new colonial possession" (1995, 54). In this sense, Cape Verde served as ground zero for the Portuguese colonial application of Lusotropicalism, which according to Brazilian sociologist Gilberto Freyre (1953) was an inherent proclivity on the part of the Portuguese for miscegenation. Cape Verdean colonial history often mirrors that of Brazil insofar as it is thought that racial prejudice was minimal and slavery was not as savage and brutal, which resulted in a "benevolent amalgamation" (Vargas 2012, 5). As a result, Portuguese colonialism is often valorized over other forms. However, as Denise Ferreira Da Silva argues in her discussion on Brazilian racial politics, a discussion that can be applied to Cape Verde, "The national discourse celebrates rape, as it postulates that the black female body was fundamental in the production of the national (racial) type; the female, the mulata, has become an *object* of national celebration, signifying both the colonizer's [*sic*] previous sexual deeds and the necessary availability of the black female body" (1998, 227). Put slightly differently, many scholars, implicitly or explicitly, sanction rape, a relation of force, as a pillar of state and cultural formation.

The application of Lusotropicalism resulted in a large *kriolu* population as well as a complex system of racial classification; a classification that would utilize skin color and other phenotypic markers like hair and nose type, a system of classification vaguely similar to the scientific study mentioned earlier.[6] Miscegenation, in turn, becomes the substance of the Cape Verdean spirit. By 1550 and throughout the following centuries the racial composition of the islands was overwhelmingly *mestiço* (Lobban 1995). Today, the official racial composition of the country is unknown, for the "race" category was dropped from the census following independence in 1975.

Although official "race" categories ceased to exist in contemporary Cape Verde, *kriolu* folk culture has distinct and overlapping racial categories, which structures the racial hierarchy. The *sampadjudo* from Sao Vincente, for instance, are considered *mulato*, but weak and feeble as a result of having African blood. Conversely, *mulato* elites look negatively on the *badiu* (meaning vagabond) not only for having African blood but also for being the bearers of African culture. The *badiu* tend to be phenotypically darker than most Cape Verdeans and are the core of the peasant population of the island of Santiago. The *badiu* with their darker skin are often viewed as the primary representatives of Africanity on the islands and, as such, have historically been denigrated by the colonial authorities and looked down upon by other Cape Verdeans including the *sampadjudo*. As Batalha as observed, "Being lighter and *sampadjudo* is also associated with being closer to the ideal of Portugueseness . . . as opposed to *badiu* Creole, which is seen as nearer to its African roots" (2004, 11). In his attempt to strengthen Cape Verdean identity and establish the principles of unification between Cape Verde and Guinea-Bissau, Amílcar Cabral spoke of the "re-Africanization of the spirit," which resulted, at times, in the *badiu* becoming a symbolic force in the fight against Portuguese colonialism and much later against neoliberalism (see Duarte 1984; Cabral 1973; Pardue 2013).

In Cape Verde the system of racial classification was and is confounded by wealth, power, island origin, and class position, which often "lightened" one's appearance, while poverty, so-called crude behavior, and illiteracy "blackened" it. An individual's race was associated not only with phenotype and corporeality, but also with one's social class and cultural capital. In this regard, this phenomenon is similar to that of Brazil. In the early twentieth century Cape Verdean racial classification and identity again was confounded by colonial decree. Complicating Cape Verdean racial classification further was the legal status *assimilado*. The status of *assimilado* was assigned to indigenous Africans in the Portuguese African colonies whose cultural standards of literacy, education, and class position would entitle them to a path to Portuguese citizenship, while the overwhelming majority of black Africans were relegated to the lowest paying jobs and inferior schools, and subjected to extralegal taxes, restricted movement, and more severe and arbitrary punishment within the criminal justice system (see Fikes 2009). In other words, the status of *assimilado* was constituted by race and culture and lent itself to justify, in law and within civil society, oppressive and violent colonial practices and policies. Further, many Cape Verdean *assimilados* complicated their position by serving as strategic intermediaries in the colonial system as local administrators and functionaries in all parts of the Luso-African world, in places like Mozambique and Angola (Lobban and Saucier 2007). Although I do not dispute the overall complexity and nuance of Cape Verdean racial history, I do not agree with Lobban when he argues that, "although Cape Verde's colonial experience was unequivocally marked by racism, social inequality, and racial stratification, any effort to impose an American, South African, or European model of racial hierarchy onto Cape Verdean society will fail" (1995, 51). While the categories used over time and space have changed, even officially vanished within the islands, blackness, which is also to say Africanity, is considered pathogenic and phobogenic (Meintel 1981), "the negative residuum of the interracial encounter" (Sexton 2008, 150). Blackness has remained foundational to Cape Verdean racial politics as it has elsewhere.

Understanding Cape Verdean racial identity becomes more complex when Cape Verdean emigration is included. Due to the country's history of persistent drought, food shortages, and poverty many Cape Verdeans, again, have immigrated to Europe and the United States. Given that more Cape Verdeans live outside Cape Verde than within, the nation has become one of emigrants. To this end, issues of racial and ethnic identity have been expanded and played out in diaspora, which marks the ways in which antiblackness is played out on a global scale. Since Cape Verdeans range in phenotype and skin color, issues of racial classification and categorization have taken on a new dynamic in the diaspora. Given the transnational nature of Cape Verdean peoples, we can also assume that the racial identity politics developed in diaspora have also impacted the ways in which Cape Verdeans in the homeland conceptualize and articulate race. Like all examples of racial identity, Cape Verdean racial subjectivity is one of contradictions and constant antagonisms. Because Cape Verdeans carried Portuguese passports and self-identified as "Portuguese" during the early and mid-twentieth century they became known in the United States as "black Portuguese," while in places like Brazil they are referred to as "black white men" (Halter 1993).[7]

Although Cape Verdeans supposedly did not fit easily into the United States' black/white binary, they were often ascribed the racial status of black, which as we will see has not changed. Being ascribed black status was something earlier settlers adamantly denounced, segregating themselves from other blacks. For example, Cape Verdean children were often discouraged from socializing with African Americans (Halter 1993). Throughout the northeast, several self-contained Cape Verdean communities existed. They published their own newspapers and newsletters (e.g., *Lebanta* and *No Pintcha*) and organized cultural and religious organizations. Cape Verdean emigrants quickly learned that being conceived of as black, regardless of being mixed race, limited their upward mobility and social standing. In other words, a basic incompatibility existed between being black and social advantage.

The immigrant voices in Halter's *Between Race and Ethnicity: Cape Verdean American Immigrants, 1860–1965* (1993) illustrate this racial understanding well. As one emigrant explained, "the first thing Cape Verdeans learn is that black people sit at the bottom of the American totem pole. We found out quickly that America doesn't believe in shade—only black and white" (quoted in Halter 1993, 146). Despite their efforts to distance themselves from African Americans and others marked as black, many Cape Verdeans were relegated to similar types of employment opportunities held by African Americans and lived in similar impoverished conditions; in a few words, they were blackened. However, Cape Verdeans were some of the first "people of color" to obtain employment in positions traditionally reserved for whites (e.g., postal worker), which may say more about the ways in which earlier diasporic populations consistently and creatively attempted to shed their Africanity and less about liberal multiculturalism in the United States (Coli and Lobban 1990). Yet in the wake of both the civil rights movement and Black Power movement, not to mention their own war of liberation, Cape Verdeans sought wider social and communal ties with African Americans. Many even embraced the term "black." Amílcar Cabral's ideas of "re-Africanizing the spirit" of all Cape Verdeans also impacted those in diaspora (see Cabral 1973). As a result, by the 1970s Cape Verdeans were especially active in the Urban League, the National Association for the Advancement of Colored People (NAACP), Congress of Racial Equality (CORE), and other national and local organizations that worked for black empowerment.

Many second-generation Cape Verdean youth actively assemble their identity at the intersection of race and other modalities of identification, negotiating notions of blackness and Cape Verdeanness (*caboverdianidade*) first and foremost. As Sánchez Gibau (2005) has shown, there exist deep tensions between immigrants and American-born Cape Verdeans about what it means to be Cape Verdean. Cape Verdeanness is exemplified generationally and contextually by certain cultural practices and reading of Cape Verdean history. To be conclusive about what it means to be Cape Verdean is futile, for it is variable, that much we cannot deny. Given their complex colonial history, geographical location, and history of migration, it is easy to assume Cape Verdeans are a multiracial people. However, processes of racialization often strip Cape Verdeans of difference and complexity; the racial hegemonic quickly absorbs difference and attempts at racial transgression, or more specifically attempts at escaping from one's blackness or Africanity (Jones 2003). In the end, historically speaking, Cape Verdean identity often objects to racism, via mixed-race metaphors, while underwriting racial rules of antiblackness.

No Room (at This Time) for Being Mixed Race

To be creole, hybrid, mixed race, or mestizo (which are all genealogically related) constitutes a political maneuver that is thought to go beyond the Manichean tendencies of modern/contemporary discourse. Being Cape Verdean, I would argue, is a political hieroglyph that requires translation. That is, Cape Verdean as synecdoche of mixed race. Therefore, previous studies on Cape Verdean identity fit well within the mixed-race movement and its intellectual offshoot, (critical) mixed race studies. It is thought that those who are mixed race, *metizo*, hybrid, creole, or some other racial amalgamation are proof of the unhinging of static differences and the deterioration of indentitarian markers. Mixed-race identities are often formulated against ontological essentialism. To be mixed race is to break from the frozen prescriptions and descriptions of the past, to be at the forefront of a new humanity (see Gilroy 2001; Hannerz 1987). In short, it is a transcendental project. Mixed race studies, critical or otherwise, are enamored with a sense of accuracy in that speaking in binary terms obliterates the reality of certain subjectivities.[8] Much of the literature also argues that the ability and right to self-identify has many benefits, one of which I would argue, *pace* Sexton (2008), is that it provides an escape from supposed outdated racial subjectivities. Or more specifically, "mixedness . . . enables black transcendence" (Joseph 2013, 26). Riffing on Ralina Joseph's insight in *Transcending Blackness: From the New Millennium Mulatta to the Exceptional Multiracial* (2013), some Cape Verdeans, particularly older ones, see themselves as "exceptional *kriolus*." Where this project differs from other work on Cape Verdean identity is that it "cuts through," what Joseph calls, "the codes of assimilationist multiracialism and calls out the anti-black racism undergirding some celebrations of mixed-race" (2013, 163).

Two trends plague the small field of Cape Verdean studies. The first trend is that Cape Verdeans reside in the break of black and white, that is, between both racial categories (Vale de Almeida 2007).[9] Sometimes it is not even an issue of being *both* black and white, but *neither* black nor white (Lima 2011). The second trend, which builds off the understanding that being Cape Verdean is neither black nor white, is that their identity is so complex that it resists categorization. For sociologist Pedro Góis, Cape Verdeanness resists empirical analysis—it is ultimately "indefinite" (2010, 274). Both trends are not accountable to blackness. In fact, present in much of the current-day grammar of Cape Verdean being, as illustrated in the brief account in the preface, is a racial ideology, a worldview that is fundamentally antiblack. Arguments against Cape Verdean blackness, like many arguments about race in the "postracial" moment, become cultural rather than racial. For many, to be Cape Verdean is an ethnocultural proclamation and designation, which is beyond the boundaries of race. As has been my experience, Cape Verdean elders, and the scholars attendant to their experiences, in many ways reverse Livio Sansone's (2003) "blackness without ethnicity" to an "ethnicity without blackness." In the United States, mixed race is often mistaken for a move toward colorblindness or racelessness. In the case of many older Cape Verdeans in the United States (and elsewhere), it is more a move away from blackness (see Challinor 2013).

Ironically, mixed-race identities, in embracing and promoting a deeper sense of self, become compatible with essentialist and identitarian thinking. What is the political nature of mixed race? Does it refer to taxonomic neutrality? In situating Cape Verdeanness within mixed race studies I am further able to point out some of the fault lines in thinking that being *kriolu* exceeds the assumptive logic of race. Upon further observation, mixed race studies is often conceptually flawed and politically inept because it only works from the register of identity and does not adequately challenge the primacy (and problem) of blackness as ontological. Not to identify as black is not to say one is not structurally positioned as black. Expression and identification with not being black have their limits, especially if one's appearance gestures toward black. Mixed race studies and other similar fields of study often fail to underline the terror and the brutal context from which the process of creolization and amalgamation was born. Thus, we need to pay attention to the mechanisms of creolization. And, in the case of Cape Verde, that mechanism was the crucible of racial slavery.

While a good deal of nuanced and forward-thinking scholarship has emerged on mixed-race people throughout the globe, many of them still lack attention to the centrality of blackness. Take, for instance, Greg Carter's *United States of the United Races: A Utopian History of Racial Mixing* (2013), where he limns at length about the instability of racial identity throughout U.S. history. Using history as his preferred method, Carter draws attention to the multiracial movement(s) of the late twentieth century and locates the precursors and antecedents of these movements in the twenty-first century. Works such as these do little to move away from the "amalgamation schemes" of the past (Sexton 2008). For Carter does not ask his reader to turn to a blackened world, meaning a more ethical world, but to the multiracial in us all. The point for Carter is not the abandonment of race, but its embrace, but the embrace is muddled and never specified. It is left unrecognized, which given the ontic relations of western modernity most likely means a turning away from blackness. For Carter, whiteness shifts, as does brownness and other racialized modalities. Racial identity over time is difficult to pin down, and to say who is or who is not black, brown, or other is an exercise in futility. If this is the case, according to Carter, we should all embrace our inner multiracial selves.

Further, when we consider mixed race studies we must examine the binary logic that functions within this discourse. Once the discourse is demystified, the binary at work is no longer the bemoaned black/white binary that supposedly obscures more than elucidates. Rather, a black/nonblack binary is at work. Declarations such as "We are more than African!" do little to eliminate antiblackness. As Sexton has argued, mixed-race declarations do "not elevate whiteness to its apex, its maximum type, or its ideal. Rather, the doctrine of white supremacy is dethroned, as a new mixed race will have superseded the white, presenting itself as that select taste toward which even the former rulers of the world aspire . . . abolish[ing] not only the reign of whiteness, but also the existence of those 'uglier stocks'—'uneducated,' 'inferior races'" (2003, 248). In other words, blackness, while often despised, is put to work, in that it is forced to labor for the mixed race, for the *kriolu* (Woods 2013).

While historically Cape Verdeanness's attendant ontology has been to eliminate blackness, the Cape Verdean youth within these pages understood with great clarity that they have "*come into being* . . . through violent acts" (Aranke 2013, 121). Derek Pardue also observed that many Cape Verdean youth in Portugal do not see their mixedness as a means to transcend blackness, but rather to be "Kriolu . . . is a sign of blackness, Africanity" (2013, 100). Amalgamation's locus classicus is understood to be rooted in racial slavery and therefore, rather than depoliticize blackness and quarantine its claims, it is politicized and embraced.

In the end, mixed race studies is a prime example of the limits of Omi and Winant's (1994) racial formation thesis. Racial formations', and by extension mixed race studies', lack is not that identities have not changed and with it new meanings and collective subjectivities, but the constitutive elements from which mixed-race identities are constructed remain, that is, the ontology of blackness as absence.

A Brief Note on the Black/Nonblack Binary

Our search for understanding through social analysis is conditioned by how we resolve several long-standing controversies, not the least of which is the relationship between black and nonblack. Racial studies, critical or otherwise, often rely on a binary conceptualization of race and racism, a black/white binary to be more exact. At times, a white/nonwhite binary is utilized so as not to conceptualize black and white as the two predominant racial categories or as the two poles for which all other racial categories are compared and analogized. Despite its popularity in the humanities and the social sciences, the black/white binary has become the subject of increased interest and scrutiny among legal and humanities scholars (see Alcoff 2006, 2013; Delgado 1998; Martinez 1998; Ortiz 2012; Perea 1997). For many, the binary, as Perea proclaimed with great reception, "dictates that all other racial identities and groups

in the United States are best understood through the Black/White binary program"
(1997, 1220). As a result, the binary is said to totally ignore (and at times even cancel
out) the presence of other people and communities of color (e.g., Asian, Creole,
Latino, Multiracial, American Indian) and by extension impede our understanding
of the depth and reach of racism in said communities. The paradigm is scandalously
understood to be an either/or proposition that discourages perceptions of common
interest and therefore promotes a divide-and-conquer strategy among people of
color (see Perea 1997). Implied in such uncharitable critiques is the problem with
blackness (see Matsuda 2002; Sundstrom 2008). Other critiques are less dogmatic
and more nuanced, but just as scandalous. The call to move beyond the black/white
binary, which really is about eliminating binary standards, can be consolidated and
generalized in the following way: the black/white binary omits and obscures the
United States' and the world's multiracial history and is unsuccessful in capturing
the historical complexity of race and racialization; all racism serves white supremacy;
the black/white binary forecloses the complexity of identity; and race is universal
and central to all western formations.

For example, philosopher Linda Alcoff (2013) argues that the black/white binary
does significant interpretive work for understanding some forms of racism but not
all forms of racism.[10] She is forthright in arguing that antiblack racism exists in "overt
and subtle ways" (Alcoff 2013, 121), but she does so only as a way to revisit the utility of the black/white binary for understanding nonblack people of color, especially
Asian American women.[11] She goes so far as to say that racism is multiple in form
but is unwilling to go as far as Charles Mills when he states, "The position of blacks
is unique among all the groups racialized as nonwhite by the modern West; for no
other nonwhite group has race been so enduringly constitutive of their identity and
so enduringly central to white racial consciousness and global racial consciousness
in general" (Mills 2013, 35). Thus, I would argue, pace Sexton (2008), that the black/
white binary, although still important, is not the binary that matters for exploring
Cape Verdean blackness. Nor is the white/nonwhite binary of any value. It might be
better to conceive of Cape Verdean blackness through not the black/white binary,
but the black/nonblack binary. To utilize the black/nonblack binary is not to say that
other forms of racism do not exist or that antiblack racism is paramount. Rather it
is simply stating that it is the bottom line, the essence, but not the totality (Sexton
2008). The black/nonblack paradigm assures a closer look at the binary opposition
between black and nonblacks.

BEING/BECOMING/BELONGING

Given the difficulty in understanding racial identity, I suggest a model for assisting us in interrogating the theoretical and material registers of racial identity among Cape Verdean youth by the triangulated articulation being/belonging/becoming. This construct gets at the complexity of black subjectivity and the ontology of race, which allows us to better map Cape Verdean youth blackness. The logic of being/belonging/ becoming highlights the fact that scholars often deal with racial identity and black subjectivity using exclusive conceptual devices, either/or proposition. Put simply, racial identity is often seen as objective or subjective, and at times intersubjective. Seldom are three combined in an effort to map racial identity. Being/belonging/becoming rethinks racial identity and race as a technology, typically theorized in piecemeal fashion, as a complex that incorporates the objective, subjective, and intersubjective. The theoretical production of being/belonging/becoming provides us with a means by which we can begin to better understand the complex sociality of blackness and its polyglot "nature." The framework being/belonging/becoming attempts to work through this impasse and interrupt and challenge, but also build on, that which has already been thematized. It demonstrates how and in what manner Cape Verdean youth blackness serves as a medium for understanding the complexity of racial antagonism in the twenty-first century, something my subjects would seldom let me forget.

Identity is complex and often means many things. Sometimes it means too little, and sometimes so much that it loses its analytical force. For some, identity is immutable and essential, and for others it is constructed as a negotiation between individuals and their environments. Rogers Brubaker and Frederick Cooper (2000) all but argue for a moratorium on its usage in social scientific studies. Instead they argue for applying three separate operations which they believe better explain what typically gets conflated as identity. First, there is categorization and self-identification. This is how others categorize people, which may be different from the ways in which they identify (see Rockquemore and Brunsma 2008). Second, there is social location and self-understanding, which explains where one fits in society and how individuals understand their (non)relations of proximity and distance from others. And, last, there is groupness, connectedness, and commonality, which all explicate the ways in which connectedness and belonging are understood.

While I agree with Brubaker and Cooper's assessment on identity, I am not ready to dispose of identity. Therefore, what I am attempting to illuminate with the framework being/belonging/becoming is that the subject is the interarticulation of these forces. In other words, Cape Verdean blackness cannot be realized and understood in separation of these three frames, for it operates as an assemblage. Although I largely omit gender and other subjectivities, I do not suggest blackness can be fully theorized without them. In fact, what is before you is a partial account and nothing more.

In the end, theoretical contributions on and about race and racial identity should be paired more aggressively with the ethnographic method. Ethnographies of identity formation allow us to focus on the ways identities are constructed and mobilized. This eliminates categorizing people into preconceived notions about how they should act and identify. This is a critical step in the elaboration of politics that take seriously black peoples', in this case second-generation Cape Verdean youths', own conceptualization of their life-world. It provides one of the only foundations upon which we can construct politics that combat the racial polity and the specifics of racial oppression and antiblackness. Cape Verdean youth at times embody a blackness that *is* the case: blackness as necessity as deterministic. At other times, Cape Verdean youth fail to *be* the case, ontology prefaced on contingency and not necessity, living in a fugue state, in "the undercommons" (see Moten 2008; Harney and Moten 2013). It doesn't have to be as it is. Identity can be, at the very least momentarily, fugitive, free from the very problem of ontology. It can also be an ethical choice. To end, I return to Rhett Jones's observation that "there have been literally millions of such people in the Americas, persons who have reflected on the meaning of blackness and decided to be black . . . [and] those who have reflected on blackness and decided not to be black" (2003, 281).

Body and Being: Notes on Cape Verdean Blackness in America

I love being black and wouldn't change for the world. If I had a choice, I would still choose black. Yeah I'm Cape Verdean, but regardless of where my family is from, I'm black.

—Informant

The work of Marilyn Halter (1993) and others clearly attempts to illustrate that early Cape Verdean immigrant identities sat between the registers of both race and ethnicity, occupying the racial middle that was again neither black nor white. However, when it comes to understanding second-generation Cape Verdean youth identity in the Greater Boston area, as the informant statement in the epigraph shows, the ambiguity and liminality surrounding race (and ethnicity) in previous generations has vanished. Cape Verdean youth have come to see themselves, racially, as black and, ethnically, as Cape Verdean. More importantly, they have come to see themselves as blacks living in an antiblack world, an abject population both locally and globally. As a result, they experience noteworthy solidarity with others racialized as black, particularly African American youth. Many of my informants informally and formally discussed the hardships their parents and grandparents endured in Cape Verde in relation to the neglected neighborhoods they inhabit, as well as the substandard schools they have attended in the United States, an implicit and explicit neglect that is ever present in an antiblack world.

Although Cape Verdean youth often reject monolithic and homogeneous definitions of blackness as an identity via the performance of their Cape Verdeanness, their identities are fundamentally structured by racial discourse. Regardless of their skin color and phenotype, second-generation Cape Verdean youth, unlike many from their parents' generation, learn to think of themselves as black with little hesitation. In fact, many strongly denounce their European ancestry, even if phenotypically apparent, in favor of the markings of blackness.[1]

As we will come to see, the consumption and production of black popular culture, particularly hip-hop, helps many Cape Verdean youth to articulate ethnic difference, while also providing them with a language and space of "reasoned comparison" with other blacks (Wacquant 2007).[2] Yet, while the consumption and production of black popular culture creates space for the performance of black difference, it also makes them subject to a more totalizing set of assumptions that they are black. Another way of putting it is that the way in which Cape Verdean youth consume and produce black popular culture is a clear illustration that blackness is also a cultural formation that is always already transnational and global (Barrett 1998). This is to say blackness is a process that produces ways of being/becoming/belonging. This chapter is about living subjectivity and the import of one's exteriority. Cape Verdean youth, in part, have become black within the anatomical economy of race. In the following pages I map, via interview material, the importance that phenotype, skin color, class, and cultural practices have in creating black identities out of difference. In this sense, what will become clear is not so much blackness as simply an identity, but the strategies of negotiating between the funk and vivacity of blackness in a world hostile to blackness.

DEFINING BLACKNESS AND THE POLITICS OF RACIAL AUTHENTICITY

What is blackness? It is an elusive concept, and to define it, as Lerone Bennett stated in his 1969 address at the first national conference of black studies directors at the Institute of the Black World, is a challenge (Bennett 1972). Blackness is overdetermined—a constituted fact—and therefore has multiple meanings, meanings rooted diachronically and synchronically. It is an identity, a historical bloc, a cultural formation, and so on (Sexton 2003). Since the invention of race, and by extension racial identity, the quest of authenticating a black identity has been a long, complex, and politically contested struggle. As an elusive racial signifier—one that is not always based solely on skin color and phenotype—blackness as an identity has sometimes been constructed as natural, one-dimensional, and static, while at other times it is multiple, a touchstone for a politics of identification (Vargas 2006). Or, as Fanon (1963) limns in *The Wretched of the Earth*, blackness is a universal standpoint for understanding not the black experience but the black condition.

Throughout this book, blackness is viewed as an identity that is part of a cultural formation that is a reflection and result of antiblackness. I straddle the dichotomous nature of blackness as fixed and multiple. On the one hand, I tease out the ways in which blackness, conceived as one-dimensional, as conforming to preexisting al-though updated patterns and stereotypes, continues to reinforce and sustain white supremacy and antiblackness. On the other hand, I repudiate the idea that there is an "authentic" undifferentiated black identity, but I am not sympathetic to calls for "postblackness." To this end, as a cultural formation, blackness incorporates certain groups of people that are engaged in some nature of cultural production, which in turn sets them in different relations with broader trends in society, relations that are often symbolically central, but ontologically and socially marginal (Sexton 2003).

As many have already argued, antiblack notions of essentialized blackness are evoked to construct and maintain essentialized notions of whiteness, but also extend to less dangerous notions of other nonblacks. The discourses of white supremacy and antiblackness have targeted and effectively marked black people as primitive, unde-serving, capricious, dangerous, unintelligent, sly, oversexed, and violent (see Fanon 1963, 1967; Hobson 2005; Sexton 2009; Sharpe 2010; Sharpley-Whiting 1999). In the past, tropes of blackness circulated in the form of Zip Coon, Stepin Fetchit, Jezebel, Sapphire, and others (see Lott 1993; Sharpley-Whiting 1999). Similarly, the discursive constructions of blackness today still represent negative and narrow depictions of blackness: the welfare queen, prison inmate, prostitute, hedonistic rapper, thug, single mother, and pimp (see Gray 2004). As a result, whiteness and nonblack people of color to a lesser extent are none of these; the trope of whiteness is supreme, pure, moral, and good. The fact of whiteness is taken as a sign of everything, rather than a sign of nothingness (Fanon 1967). In the end, whiteness is everything blackness is not, thus the need not necessarily to be white, but at least not to be black. As Fanon (1967) demonstrated, racism and constructions of blackness are interrelated, particularly because the cultural formation is antiblack. And David Theo Goldberg stands correct when he states "blackness has been produced in coercive circumstances" (1997, 75), that is, produced in the crucible of slavery and the plantation and their surrogate sociocultural formations. Blackness has been constructed within a culture of racialized preclusion from state and civil society. In attending to various types and modalities of blackness, we must not forget that while blackness is often constructed as nonhuman or subhuman, black people are indeed human (Moten 2008).

Essentialized notions of blackness come not only from the outside—from white and nonblack people—but also from black people, which illustrates the force of anti-blackness in its ability to create a structure of feeling that is antithetical to their being in the world. As Raymond Williams recommends in *Marxism and Literature* (1977), we must attend to both the internal and external organization of cultural formations. For example, the negritude movement of the twentieth century attempted to rescue blackness from the racist and colonial gaze and as a result provided inspiration for and unity among black people. However, it simply inverted the terms of colonial and racist discourse. As evidenced by thinkers like Leopold Senghor, the negative associations of blackness were rarely questioned; rather they were redeployed as positive. In other words, some negritude writers and thinkers continued to rely on white hegemonic stereotypes of blackness as identity, as evidenced by Fanon in *The Wretched of the Earth* (1963).

As bell hooks observed in her essay "Postmodern Blackness (1990)," many black people uphold essentialized notions of blackness and thus are unwilling to accept the multiplicity of blackness because they "fear that it will cause folks to lose sight of the specific history and experience of African-Americans and the unique sensibilities and culture that arise from that experience" (hooks 1990). For hooks, blackness exists outside the context of essentialism; it exists beyond the oppositional and reductive gaze of whiteness. Similarly, Greg Tate limns at length about black identity.

> Perhaps the supreme irony of black American existence is how broadly black people debate the question of cultural identity among themselves while getting branded as a cultural monolith by those who would deny us the complexity and complexion of a community, let alone a nation. If Afro-Americans have never settled for the racist reductions imposed upon them—from chattel slaves to cinematic stereotype to sociological myth—it's because the black collective conscious not only knew better but also knew more than enough ethnic diversity to subsume these fictions. (quoted in Kelley 1997, 15)

Similarly, the late Marlon Riggs underscored the multiplicity of blackness in relationship to constructs of identity. He illustrated through films like *Tongues Untied* (1989) and *Black Is... Black Ain't* (1994) that when people attempt to define what it is to be black, they delimit its possibilities. That is, the pursuit of an "authentic" blackness, one rooted in conventional forms, confines and restricts black subjects and therefore human potentiality. For Riggs, blackness needs to be seen as a site of complexity and endless possibility.[3] Part of the complexity and (im)possibility in blackness is that it is not an either/or proposition (Moten 2003). That is, essentialist notions of blackness must be understood as one part of the negotiation of being in an antiblack world; essentialist tropes are not evidence of an "essence," but rather patterns of those expressions. Again, there is a difference between blackness and black people and what they choose to do with such haunting notions of what is and what isn't black.

Ron Eglash's (1999) work on African fractals offers another way of thinking about black identitarian complexity. In looking at African aesthetic designs, Eglash has found that there are essentially five geometric elements to all African design in metalwork, hairstyles, and quantitative techniques, among other things. While not conflating my work with some geometric equation, I do feel that the construction, performance of, and engagement with blackness that Cape Verdean youth exhibit is in many ways fractal. Eglash's five elements are recursion, scaling, self-similarity, infinity, and fractional dimensions. Recursion is the process of repetition. In this sense, the output of blackness becomes the input for the reproduction of blackness. Scaling suggests that variations do not follow linear lines, that is, blackness is simultaneously diachronic and synchronic. Self-similarity refers to the ways in which patterns do not have to be identical in order to qualify as part of the same thing. In other words, blackness does not always have to look the same in order for it to be blackness. Infinity illustrates that variations are infinite, that is, blackness either here or there will vary; there exists no finitude; blackness has no limit, hence it is without guarantee. Using fractional dimensions to understand blackness we can conclude that blackness is not whole, but fractions of other relationships; it is the triangulation of being/becoming/belonging. Blackness in this sense is not some occult force that binds blacks together naturally; it is "not a particular band of wave-lengths" but the interaction and engagement, willingly or unwillingly, with "a particular structural position" (Mills 2013, 33).

In his book *We Who Are Dark: The Philosophical Foundations of Black Solidarity* (2005), Tommie Shelby conceptualizes blackness as a political subjectivity that features both a thin and a thick form. Thus Shelby provides "a basis for black political unity that does not deny, downplay, or disparage individual or group differentiation within the black population" (2005, 3). Thin blackness is based solely on skin color, phenotype, and ancestry, the substance for one's structural position. For Shelby, "One cannot simply refuse to be thinly black. . . . No amount of wealth, income, social status, or education can ease one's thin blackness" (2005, 208). In other words, one is visibly marked. John McClendon's minimalist definition of blackness is strikingly similar to Shelby's definition of thin blackness. For McClendon (2005), blackness as a social category rests on both phenotypic description and genotypic classification. Phenotypic description highlights the decisiveness of the body, while genotypic classification amends the phenotypic crisis caused by race mixing by establishing one's origin of descent. A thick conception of blackness includes physical characteristics, genealogy, and more.

The more includes ideas about cultural heritage, nationality, ethnicity, kinship, and "an identifiable ensemble of beliefs, values, conventions, traditions, and practices that is distinctively black" (Shelby 2005, 211).[4] According to Shelby, persons who satisfy the thin social criteria for blackness can and often do embrace thick conceptions of blackness. Blackness is a political and analytical term in that it speaks of the lived experience of blacks and is a way in which to frame the black community across geographical boundaries. However, this embrace varies in intensity and commitment.

Regardless of transgression (deviation from the mean of essentialized blackness) or an embrace of thick conceptions of blackness, as Frantz Fanon described in *Black Skin, White Masks* (1967), there is "the lived experience of blackness." No matter what, despite his objection to an essential and thin blackness, Fanon states, "I was responsible at the same time for my body, for my race, for my ancestors. . . . I discovered my blackness . . . and I was battered down by tom-toms, cannibalism, intellectual deficiency, fetishism, racial defects, slave ships, and above all else, above all: 'Sho' good eatin'" (Fanon 1967, 112). Both the historical-racial schema (the sedimentation of experience that one endures) and the epidermal-racial schema (the internal horizon of the self) come to the fore, creating a certain kind of facticity of blackness.

Despite "the lived experience of blackness," black identity relies on the ongoing process of performance and negotiation. Notions of racial authenticity are achieved through cultural production and performative practices. Blackness is a lived project, a project that entails commitments on the part of actors (Yancy 2005). Typically, racial authenticity involves an assessment of the degree to which someone is intelligible to others. Any attempt to speak of black authenticity is an attempt to draw the boundaries of blackness as a racial signifier. In other words, common forms of racial authenticity confine the social actor in how he or she can *act* or *be* in the world. Such an idea squares well with Barnor Hesse's concept of "raceocracy." He uses the term "raceocracy" to refer to the following:

> The way in which race orders the political and social lives of people—without being accountable to any spoken or written discourse, simply because it's performed as a shared social and institutional orientation. In other words, it's racially performed in such a way that it sustains a broad range of people's relationships by facilitating conventional aspects of life that everybody appears to agree upon. (quoted in Burtenshaw 2012)

To this end, the inclusion and exclusion of subjects from blackness is political and never innocent, for the drawing of boundaries is always political. That is, it always says something about the culture of politics. Racial authenticity can be read as a way of establishing social credibility while also protecting interests, whatever those interests may be. When we engage in questions around racial authenticity, we are asking what it means to be of a particular race. We are asking how these identities/subjectivities are constructed and by whom.

As Shelley Eversley has observed, "racial authenticity is masquerading as the natural, ontological 'truth' about people of color" (2004, 79). Racial authenticity pervades black culture in that the "real" or "authentic" becomes a cultural stance, a racial positionality, an index of culture, and a barometer of trust of racial group members. In chapter 1 ("Looking for the Real Nigga") of *Yo' Mama's Disfunktional!* (1997), Robin D. G. Kelley illustrates with ease and sophistication how social scientists over time have created ethnographies about "authentic Negroes" and collapsed the experiences of black people into one monolithic experience (see Judy 1994; Neal 2013). These same social scientists in turn constructed the image that black urban areas, known as the ghetto, were thought to be monolithic geographic spaces.[5] These studies and others that followed were persistent on looking "for that elusive 'authentic' ghetto sensibility, the true, honest, unbridled, pure cultural practices that capture the raw, ruffneck 'reality' of urban life" (Kelley 1997, 35). As Gordon argues, "One doesn't *ask* a black; one *concludes* about him" (2000, 162). For many, that reality can now be found in the practices and forms of hip-hop culture and more specifically rap music, the so-called authentic, unmediated voice of urban ghetto youth (see Neal 2013; Young 2012). Similarly, as Essex Hemphill explained in *Black Is . . . Black Ain't* "Perhaps the standard . . . is the inner city for defining what blackness is. That you've got to constantly be up on the changes in the hip language, the hip black fashions, the hip black music. You've got to use your ghetto experience as your American Express Card." In other words, "the ghetto," is a prerequisite to the "real" black experience (Forman 2001). Herein lies a problem with connecting racial authenticity with experience, for it omits insight into the black condition as a whole.

It can be argued that racial authenticity as an analytical concept has been overused, and as a result scholarly analysis of racialized phenomena is shortsighted because of its reliance on the concept. Anthropologist John L. Jackson (2005) questions the validity of authenticity as a conceptual analytic stating that it stunts a fuller understanding of racial identity and black identity in particular. To pair racial sincerity with racial authenticity creates a framework for understanding blackness and those classified as black. Racial sincerity as a conceptual analytic urges researchers to look at the efforts of the participants in order to see how they get on with their everyday lives. It allows one to deal with the intellectual space between objects and the lived experience. Put slightly differently, racial sincerity allows us to look at constructions of blackness and how actual black people negotiate said constructions (Moten 2008). Unlike commonly and promiscuously used forms of racial authenticity, racial sincerity highlights the *intent* of social actors, not the *content* of the social actor. In other words, racial sincerity is about the logic, rationales, and motives that people attribute to aspects of their own *being* (ontology) and to others (Jackson 2005). However, I do not think this distinction between racial authenticity and racial sincerity, although useful, is necessary if one returns to more traditional forms of defining racial authenticity as evidenced by Bennett's (1972) "challenge of blackness." Racial authenticity in its more traditional sense, not the tendentious and essentialized way in which many use it, is really about challenging problematic constructions of blackness and the racial hierarchy. As Monahan states:

> Racial authenticity means a constant critical reflection on one's relationship to the political mechanisms of race-making and racialized intersubjectivity. . . . Racial authenticity is thus at every turn a demand for political commitment. It is an effort to be true to oneself—an interrogation of how social reality conditions who we are as individual agents, and our own particular contributions to that reality. (Monahan 2005, 48)

Authenticity, through Du Boisian "spiritual strivings," attempts to find "a better and truer self" through critical self-reflection. Through self-reflection one is able to transcend, even if momentarily, the confinement of being an object (see Césaire 2000; Moten 2003, 2008). Through self-discovery comes self-creation. To this end, authentic blackness identifies with various aesthetic, moral, physical, and cognitive categories and implications. Blackness is in many ways an ethical identity that is not always tied to pigmentation. Blackness in this sense is rooted in liberation (Bennett 1972). Blackness while imposed is a choice, for one must choose to politically engage, just as Cape Verdean youth have chosen to not be Cape Verdean first, an issue I will take up shortly. As Molefi Asante asserts, "To do blackness is to participate in an assertive program of human equality, indeed, affirmative behavior to eradicate doctrines of white supremacy" (2005, 215). In other words, blackness is an honorable commitment, a signifier of insurgent meaning.

As I will show, when Cape Verdean youth are marked as "black" and in turn become black they do so with varying intensity, engagement, and commitment. That is, what many of my informants highlighted over and again was a willingness to *be* black, that is, "to 'be' black—not in terms of convenient fads of playing blackness, but by paying the social costs of antiblackness on a global scale" (Gordon 1997, 67).

THE LIVED EXPERIENCE OF CAPE VERDEAN BLACKNESS

In an antiblack world, blackness is often associated with disadvantage, criminality, and more generally pathology. Thus black immigrants have and often seek to distance themselves from such associations. In turn, many use ethnicity as an important marker of distinction.[6] This tactic is particularly useful for black immigrants, for it is difficult to deny thin blackness, but denying thick forms of blackness, especially those rooted in culture and cultural practices, is less difficult. Historically, the children of black immigrants have "merged" into black American populations (Abdullah 2009; Clark 2008; Greer 2013; Foner 2013; Waters 1994, 2001). Tekel Woldemikael (1989) distinguishes between first- and second-generation Haitian immigrants in Illinois. Woldemikael found that the first generation maintained a strong ethnic national identity, while Haitians become culturally black Americans in the second generation. This is recapitulated in Alex Stepick's (1998) research on second-generation Haitians in Miami. In her study of Afro-Caribbean immigrants in New York City, sociologist Mary Waters (1994) found that second-generation immigrants from families of higher economic status maintained a strong ethnic-national identity, while those from lower-income neighborhoods and poor families adopt African American identities, that is, their language is influenced by black popular culture, as are their cultural tastes and perceptions of race and racism. Yndia Lorick-Wilmot's (2007) study on Caribbean immigrants reinforces the importance of community and social organization in ethnic identity construction and maintenance. Other research shows that the children of immigrants, rather than sever ties with their homeland, engage in transnational practices, that is, maintain socioeconomic and political ties to the homeland (see Levitt and Waters 2002).

For second-generation Cape Verdean youth, blackness is central to identity formation (see Ibrahim 2014). While the parents and grandparents of Cape Verdean youth commonly sought to resist racial ascription or a particular form of racial ascription, that is, blackness, today's youth do not. It can be argued that the investment in antiblackness exhibited by older Cape Verdeans was a way in which to validate their European descent or nonblackness. It was a way to distinguish them from the inferiority imposed on the black, while advancing their closeness, hence their humanness, to the white. Cape Verdeans bought into the invention of blackness by the European and its attendant negativity. It was a way in which to sever their relation to blackness and designated inferiorities. They were in many ways attempting to pass as mixed and hence as a new person, or at least transcend being black (see Joseph 2013; Sexton 2008; Zack 1993). Rather than distance themselves from African American youth many of my informants have extensive contact with African American youth and black popular culture. In Fanonian terms, many Cape Verdean youth understand the "lived experience of blackness" as the following interview excerpts illustrate.[7]

PKS: How do you identify in terms of race and ethnicity?

ANTONIO: Personally, I identify with being back. I'm black! I'm a black man!

PKS: Do you identify with any ethnicity?

ANTONIO: Again, I'm black, but ethnically I'm Cape Verdean. Being Cape Verdean takes a back seat to being black.

PKS: Why does it take a backseat?

ANTONIO: Black is first because that is what you see. Look at my skin color and how I dress. People don't know I'm Cape Verdean. Plus, that wouldn't make a difference. Black and white is too powerful of a concept. You look at me you'll say I'm black.

Another informant, again, when asked how he identifies in terms of race and ethnicity, while loosely identifying with being Cape Verdean, also emphatically stated, "I'm black!" "Look bro,'" he said, "you ain't fooling anyone to say you're not black. Yeah, I can say I'm Cape Verdean or African or whatever, but what will that do? Tell the police that shit. The fact is I'm black, if I like it or not."

Despite claiming Cape Verdean identities these two informants understand that it means little in a society where race and antiblackness are at the vortex of society's creation. Thus my participants' claims are at odds with Halter who states "For the Cape Verdean American, social identity can never be assumed and is never given" (1993, 174). Despite efforts, at times, to transcend racial categorization, Cape Verdeans, whether they approve or disapprove, are sucked into the vortex of the racial state. In this case, Cape Verdeans are both contingently and necessarily black (Gordon 2000). Black racial identity is coercive in part because identity formation is coercive. They suffer from what philosopher Charles Mills (1998) has rightfully identified as "the stigmata of subordination," due to the mark of blackness.

In the focus group that I conducted, Soraya from Tauton, Massachusetts, via Brockton, Massachusetts, had this to say about being black: "No one has ever considered me a white person. They always say 'Yeah, that's that black girl.'" Carlos, a twenty-two-year-old native of Brockton, Massachusetts, and proud Cape Verdean, had the following to say after explaining how his parents, especially his mother, ironically identified as black.

PKS: Do you also consider yourself black?

CARLOS: Yes, I do.

PKS: What's first? Black or Cape Verdean?

CARLOS: To me, if you put anything *before* black in America you're fooling yourself. Because they don't care if you been here ten years or whatever. All they know is you're a nigga!

Eighteen-year-old Juvenal of Providence, Rhode Island, echoes Carlos's sentiments.

PKS: How do you identify in terms of race and ethnicity?

JUVENAL: I say I'm black, but the weird thing is a lot of Cape Verdeans won't say they're African, but that's what we are. Cape Verdeans are African, they're black, but at the same time we're mixed. And a lot of first-generation Cape Verdeans, like my mother, identify as European. She has difficulty identifying as African . . .

PKS: But—[interrupted by Juvenal]

JUVENAL: Here, I'm black. My parents never said to me "you're black." They said, "you're Cape Verdean!" But if you live here long enough that don't matter.

In answering similar questions, Nino passionately asserted:

Those who assert their Cape Verdeanness are tip-toeing around blackness. They just don't want to get close to the idea that they are a bunch of abandoned sub-Saharan Negroes. Being Cape Verdean is life support for the dead. Being mixed circumvents the violence of white supremacy. Yeah see, when I'm positioned as black there is the struggle to say I'm Cape Verdean. Cape Verdean is an attempt to escape blackness. The policeman with the gun to my head doesn't give a fuck I'm Cape Verdean. Being 40 percent this or that, when my skin says black, doesn't matter!

Being Cape Verdean in a world where race is of central importance simply means being assigned to an unfavorable position in the racial hierarchy. In his concern over the celebration of hybrid identities, much like Fanon's concern over the praise for "negritude," Peter McLaren states: "We are not autonomous citizens who can fashionably choose whatever ethnic [and racial] combinations we desire in order to reassemble our identity . . . it is dishonest to assert that pluralized, hybridized identities are options" (1997, 7). Despite seeming deterministic, McLaren's observation reflects what many of my informants stated in informal and formal interviews: the friction between the common understanding that race and racial identity is produced through discursive regimes of power and black ontology as a given.

Throughout many of my interviews, I sensed from my informants a yearning to simply be "Cape Verdean," but as many noted this is difficult, if not impossible, in an antiblack world. As Anthony, a twenty-one-year-old born in Pawtucket, Rhode Island, of Cape Verdean parents, stated: "Society makes you black. Being Cape Verdean is second, if it means anything at all."[8] In short, some Cape Verdean youth treat blackness as totalizing in which ethnicity, culture, and ancestry are undifferentiated, subsumed under the structural position of blackness. That is, they become secondary in a world of ontological dispossession.

SIMILARITIES, DIFFERENCES, AND SOLIDARITY IN BLACKNESS

Many informants related to being black, which for some is coterminous with being African, and were careful to draw a distinction between being African and African American. Many did not identify as African American (or black American), but identified through a "reasoned comparison" with African Americans and their experiences (Wacquant 2007). Living in an antiblack social world forces one to desire and work for group solidarity, to be a community rather than a collection or bunch of objects (Judy 1994). Herein I define solidarity loosely, for it is not meant to be a comprehensive political program, although it can be, nor is it meant to address every social problem black people experience. Rather, solidarity, as it is alluded to below, is based on the shared racial condition of being black in an antiblack world.

Having lived in the Greater Boston area for the better part of her twenty-three years, Luisa offered the following insight into Cape Verdean identity.

> PKS: How do you define yourself?
> LUISA: I'm black and Cape Verdean.
> PKS: What makes you black?
> LUISA: My ancestors and the conditions under which we often live.
> PKS: Anything else?
> LUISA: Yeah . . . background, skin color, and culture.
> PKS: What do you mean by background and culture?
> LUISA: All our dances and rituals come from Africa. For example, *batuko* and *funana* are both African. As for background, I'm *badius*.

Here it is important to note that the *badius*, descendants from runaway slaves on the island of Santiago, are a people that have retained a certain degree of Africanity in their cultural practices from other Cape Verdeans; the *badius*, again, were of great symbolic importance during the war of liberation. Luisa also stated: "I'm black, but I'm not African American. When I think of African Americans, their traditions are different. I mean they have jazz and the blues. We got *funana*. Do we have similarities? Sure! Like our struggle with racism. It's because of racism that we should unite as a people." While Luisa accepts her blackness, she is resolute in drawing a distinction between "black" as a racial identity and African American, seeing the latter as culturally distinct from Cape Verdeans such as herself.

While identifying as black Cape Verdean, Carlos offers this lengthy insight into similarities and solidarity with black Americans:

Like I said before, I do identify with black Americans because unlike continental Africans—even though for some of them they've been moved around. People think because they're from Ghana or whatever their family was always there, but not necessarily because people were moved throughout the slave trade. And Cape Verde was uninhabited. Once you get back to Cape Verde you don't know where you go. And Cape Verde was founded around the same time the American colonies were getting Africans. So our history probably goes back as far as theirs. So for me I identify with that. Our histories are similar. [Pause] So when people go, well at least you know what country you're from. Well, not really. Cape Verde wasn't there before. So I identify with that. . . . So first of all I identify with them [African Americans] in terms of black issues and what should be of concern for us as a people in terms of where we are and where we're lagging. [Pause] I think also being black or feeling black, I think maybe I have a hypersensitivity to race. Sometimes people will say, "You're just looking for prejudice. Maybe they were just having a bad day." But being black you don't have that luxury, being a black person in America, if you're conscious of history. You can walk around with your blinders on and say "its equal. And I'm going to get a job like anybody else and I didn't get it because the other guy was more qualified." Simply put! You can believe that if you want to, but if you are cognizant of the civil rights movement, if you're cognizant of slavery, and anything that has happened since then. I'd rather welcome that and put that in my backpack. Being black is something I can't control. And that's why I think I'm so problack. . . . I mean I don't believe in racial superiority. I'm not a black supremacist. Me loving black doesn't mean I'm hating anybody else. . . . Problackness is antiwhiteness. I think this is how it is perceived in this country. Whereas I think it's different. I'm problack. That doesn't mean I hate white people or whatever.

Carlos's identification with African Americans is based on a historical fact that most African Americans know little about which specific parts of Africa their ancestors came from. Further, he highlights the shared structural position of black youth in the United States. Due to this he feels he has more in common (culturally) with African American youth than African youth, despite understanding that structural racism affects both groups. Throughout his interview he grouped African Americans and Cape Verdeans by using the first person plural pronoun "we." Carlos's use of the pronoun "we" is significant and draws attention to the structural and historical similarities of "black people." For Carlos, racial discrimination was historically directed uniformly at individuals of African descent, regardless of difference. Blackness is the base for many Cape Verdean youth in the Greater Boston area in their attempt to find an effective structure of sociality. While commenting on the crisis of the postcolonial moment, sociologist Paget Henry has observed that the complementary subjectivities of "I" and "we" "must be reinforced by similarities or convergences between discourses, symbols, and ideals." For Henry, the "I" and "we" "are sites of freedom, volition, the capacity for making claims through dialogue" (2007, 46). The "we," it can be argued, grounds the identity in a community of blackness, politically constituted in struggle. Cape Verdean youth, at least those that I met and talked with, attempt to do their part to help reanimate blackness as a vehicle of collective and political mobilization.

Born in Providence, Rhode Island, Francisco, a twenty-four-year-old second-generation Cape Verdean, also emphasizes experiential similarities and as a result the need for solidarity:

> FRANCISCO: A small number of Cape Verdeans in America don't seem to like to be identified as black or African American. . . . We should be aware of the fact that as, we say in *crioulo*, "a união faz força" [united we are strong] and stop trying not to identify with black people because that is what we are, either black Africans or black Americans for those born in America.
>
> PKS: Can you say more?
>
> FRANCISCO: Yes, we are Cape Verdeans, but we are still black people. . . . I mean where did we come from? West Africa! What is the predominant race and culture of Cape Verde? African people and African culture! Just because we have some Portuguese blood in us doesn't mean we're not black. How many black people don't have some European blood? So, let's be proud of who we are: black and African!

Cape Verdean youth experiences with antiblackness, not to mention antiblack racism, lead them to see themselves as black and African. Antiblackness prompts self-defining cultures of resistance. As anthropologist Joao Costa Vargas has observed, "as much as black bodies are subjected to dehumanization, they also perform counter-narratives that, although not always effective in negating the imposed norms, nevertheless suggest possibilities beyond . . . antiblackness." He continues to argue that resistance is "as much about psychic survival as they are about symbolic reconfiguration and political experimentation" (2012, 8). As a result, they experience solidarity with other marked black bodies particularly African Americans and continental Africans, who they see as inhabiting the same social position in the U.S. and global antiblack structure. Some Cape Verdeans draw cultural distinctions between Cape Verdeans and African Americans, choosing instead to identify with continental Africans. What should also be highlighted is that second-generation Cape Verdean youth do not deploy ethnicity to draw a distinction from blackness, but to complicate blackness as an identity. The deployment of "Africa" and "African" is presented as a political project. Therefore, they are not obfuscating the power relations embedded in processes of racialization. My informants articulate a desire for a Pan-African politics of liberation that comes from similar experiences of oppression and racialization. We should be clear that this desire for solidarity does not cancel out individual autonomy or growth.

In the end, my informants express a connected fate with African Americans, a shared history of oppression rooted in ideologies of white supremacy and antiblackness that has motivated these youth to develop a common narrative of preclusion and struggle, and a shared consciousness. Given this, racial belonging is important for group mobilization—social issues become framed as important for the "black" community, locally and globally, a part of which many of my informants see themselves. Here I think Cape Verdean youth are correct contra Kwame Anthony Appiah and Amy Gutman's (1996) concern that solidarity undermines individual autonomy. Since antiblackness is not geared toward individuals but a group, as More echoing Biko (2002) has observed, "it is impossible to fight racism as an autonomous individual" (More 2009, 35). Put differently, living in an antiblack world solicits the political ontology of blackness.

A Note on Mistaken Identity

Despite identifying with other racially marked subjects like African Americans and continental Africans, the Cape Verdean youth that I interviewed resisted identification with other nonblack people of color, particularly Latinos. This may say something about the limited utility within and outside academic circles of the conflated category "people of color" and the need for the use of the more honest configuration "nonblack people of color." Given their tendency to be light in skin color and to speak a "foreign" language, which to the untrained ear might sound like Spanish, Cape Verdeans are often mistaken as Dominican or Puerto Rican; both groups constitute sizable populations in the Greater Boston area. As one informant noted with slight dismay: "Some people think I'm Hispanic. . . . I always get, 'are you Puerto Rican? Are you Dominican?'" In this context, my informants were adamant about defining their Cape Verdeanness and blackness as exhibited by the following statement: "I always let people know I'm a black Cape Verdean. I don't want to be mistaken for nobody else." In her study on Cape Verdeans in Boston, Sánchez Gibau (2005) suggests that there exist between Cape Verdeans and Latinos great similarities, culturally and socially, which has resulted in a relationship between the Latino population and Cape Verdean diaspora. She speaks of a sense of affinity in life experiences, based both on foreign status and language issues. This may be the case with previous generations and current immigrants, or the promiscuous use and conflation of all nonwhite people, but for my informants it was not. Rather, my informants were resolute in denying any relationship to Latinos. This resistance to being identified as Latino raises questions of immigration and citizenship. Cape Verdean youth of the Greater Boston area resist this form of Latino classification by defining themselves as black and/or Cape Verdean. Through this act, not only are black and/or Cape Verdean identities claimed, but also a form of citizenship.

There are complexities and problems with a word like citizenship, for it is used in a number of different ways in academic and political discourse and social contexts. Herein I am not referencing a citizenship that takes on the specific juridical links between individual and state. Rather, I use citizenship in a simple way to mean belonging to a national community and "a set of moral qualities thought to be crucial for the existence of the good citizen" (Martiniello 2002, 116).

Unlike assimilation theories of the past, Ana Ramos-Zayas (2007) has shown that "becoming American" for Brazilian and Puerto Rican youth of Newark is not necessarily tied with "becoming white." Rather, she shows that migrants from Latin America associated blackness with "Americanness." Given my informants' incessant need to draw a distinction between themselves and Latinos, I suggest, much like Ramos-Zayas (2003, 2007), that there is an alternative way of exerting and claiming citizenship. This reversal of citizenship or assimilationist logic is a move, according to Ramos-Zayas, away from "delinquent" forms of citizenship. Although previous generations attempted to assert their belonging via "acting white" or drawing a sharp distinction between Cape Verdeans and blacks, today's youth attempt to belong by embodying blackness, by the valorization of blackness and the devalorization of anything other.

According to my informants, Cape Verdean youth are often confused for "being Latino." As Juvenal, who identifies as black and Cape Verdean, stated:

> I get "you're Spanish," "you're Dominican" all the time. In high school all the girls would come up to me speaking Spanish. People will argue with me until the death saying I'm Dominican. But I always make sure I tell people I'm a black Cape Verdean. . . . I don't like being called any other ethnicity.

The denunciation and adamant responses of distinctiveness from being Latino could be a deliberate way to escape the stigma associated with "immigrant." Being an immigrant often conjures images of illegality. Further, it suggests backwardness and foreignness. Denouncing their perceived Latinoness, while aligning themselves with black people, Cape Verdean youth escape the negative connotations of "immigrantness" especially following the heightened nativism of 9/11 and the subsequent war on terror. In avoiding an immigrant identity one transcends the ambiguity of liminality and not belonging. Or it could be a reasoned response to the ways in which Latinos, at times, have made legible their humanity in relation to blackness as deviant and undeserving (see Cacho 2012). However there were times when informants, although ironically, did not mind being confused for Latino. As Nino sarcastically remarked, "When people think I'm Puerto Rican, which happens all the time, I'm like good! My life expectancy increases. I'll be jailed less. Life gets better."

Spatial Narratives of Cape Verdean Blackness

Racial identity as many scholars have illustrated is not predicated solely on skin color and phenotype. It is also imbued with social significance like "space (locale)" and "place (the realities of physical terrain)." For Forman and others "the term 'inner-city' implicitly refers to racialized images or racially infected conditions of danger, violence, and depravity that can be contrasted with the ideals of calm, safety, and security attributed to non-urban or suburban space" (Forman 2001, 43). Interestingly, the relationship between race and geography has shifted from largely a rural concern to an urban concern (see McKittrick 2011). With this shift in concern came a shift in the locus of moral panic (Goldberg 2002). Du Bois's *Philadelphia Negro* (1899 [1996]), which prefigured Drake and Cayton's *Black Metropolis* (1962), and the work of Robert Park and the Chicago School signaled a change in the ecological foci of social scientists from the countryside to city. Simultaneously, racial state policies shifted their focus of containment and spatial segregation from the rural to the urban. These transformations did not occur out of simple curiosity; rather they were the result of black migration north. The more black urbanization expanded, the more racial segregation and restriction of black residents within cities was extended. As a result, not only did regions become racialized, neighborhoods became racially and ethnically segregated. As Nancy Denton (1994), Mike Davis (2006), and many others have pointed out, black segregation in urban communities is not the result of black housing preferences but of conscious white avoidance and state design. What emerged is a strong connection between blackness and urban space in that the symbolic value of the "inner city" now screams black subjectivity in the conventional and essentialized sense.

For my informants, urban communities, "the hood," and inner cities are black spaces. In other words, they are spaces occupied by black people including themselves. When asked where they were from and what their neighborhood was like, many of my participants became extremely specific, identifying specific streets and historical markers (namely project housing complexes), even recalling house numbers at times. I must admit, at first I thought the hyperspecificity was strange and unimportant, especially given that my informants were to remain anonymous and any reference to where they lived seemed almost to violate ethical codes. I later realized that the distinctions my informants seemingly wanted to draw were to differentiate who lived *where*. For instance, if the city itself was not predominantly black, certain streets and sections of town were racialized. The following statements from various informants suggest this:

I don't live in the good section like the East Side. . . . I live, and have all of my life, lived in the hood. Ya' know the Southside, near the projects.

Let's get it straight. East Providence is predominantly white, but all my neighbors were African American or Cape Verdean. In Pawtucket, the same thing.

I'm not from the best neighborhood. I mean I'm from South Providence. Crime is high and the cops are everywhere.

Where I'm from, things are difficult. People are surviving day by day. The ghetto is a hard place to grow up in.

Basically, my entire neighborhood was all black. There were a couple of Spanish people on my block, but that's it. . . . The funny thing is all around us it's nice.

My neighborhood, which is mostly black and Latino, is not the best neighborhood in the world; people selling drugs, getting shot. A lot happens! There is a lot of crime. . . . Poverty is high. Even the white people in the neighborhood are poor.

I grew up in Dorchester in "Cape Verde-vill" from Bowden Street all the way to Dudley.

The streets I lived on in Roxbury, everybody was Cape Verdean. But when I moved to Taunton, everybody was white except the Puerto Ricans and black people on my block.

In relation to the first and third statements, the racial and ethnic breakdown of South Providence, for instance, also known affectionately at times by its inhabitants as the "Southside," is 41 percent Latino and 34 percent black or African American. Nearly one-third of families in the area live below the poverty line and receive some form of public assistance. The area continues to struggle with poverty issues; the South Side's median family income is $24,656 as compared with $32,058 for the city of Providence as a whole, and more than one out of three families live in poverty. Conversely, the East Side is the most affluent part of the city of Providence with higher property values, lower unemployment, and higher income levels than the city as a whole. The College Hill area, located on the East Side, for example, is predominately white, with only 5 percent of families living below the poverty line. The median family income of the College Hill area is over $100,000. There is no doubt that most of my informants lived and continue to live in markedly racial space and places.[9]

Of participants who moved, many moved from urban community to urban community. Although the place differed the space remained similar, often highlighting the deep and intimate connect between race and class position. Informants seemed to maintain that blackened subjects, like Cape Verdeans, live in segregated communities and areas with little interracial contact (Massey and Denton 1989; Massey 2008). For example, despite movement to other locales, racial and class demographics were alike, housing and school systems comparable. Some informants described circular urban migratory patterns, such as being born in Pawtucket, growing up in East Providence, only to move back to Pawtucket during adolescence. This phenomenon highlights a reversal in Cape Verdean settlement patterns. Cape Verdeans have gone from voluntary segregation, that is, consciously living away from African Americans so as not to be identified with them, to involuntary segregation, to now living within African American communities.

With the exception of two, the Cape Verdean youth I interviewed lived and continue to live in urban areas. Interesting, and what made me realize the importance of space, particularly racialized spaces like the "inner city," were the two who spent some time growing up in a white suburban enclave in Massachusetts but who valorized being from "the hood" or the inner city.

Even those who spent the early part of their childhood in Cape Verde, particularly in the urban cities of Mindelo and Praia, highlighted to me the decrepit conditions into which they were born. As one participant who was born in the area of Praia known as the "Plateau" stated, "I've always been from the hood." Even though many have not returned since leaving or maintain little contact with family members in the islands, many emphasized the city's seemingly worsening harsh conditions. These informants almost fetishized the conditions and realities of Cape Verde's urban enclaves.

Why valorize the hood or "being urban"? Here social scientist Pierre Bourdieu's (1984) definition of "cultural capital" is instructive, for the valorization of "being urban" is a means of bringing sociocultural distinction to one's black identity; it is part of the performative aspect of being black. In a sense, what many Cape Verdean youth have projected and take pride in is a "streetwise" presentation of self. In his book *Streetwise: Race, Class, and Change in an Urban Community* (1992), Elijah Anderson suggests that being streetwise is a way to navigate the harsh realities of urban America. While this can be said for those Cape Verdean youth who spent their lives in urban communities, what does it mean when those who have spent time away from urbanity continue to valorize "being urban"? And why would some participants valorize the harsh conditions of Cape Verdean cities?

I want to suggest that "being urban" is at the vortex of the Greater Boston area blackness.[10] Being black is to be of a particular space and, by extension, specifically classed. Nino, for instance, declared more than once, "Being poor is just an everyday reminder of blackness." In her study on Brazilian and Puerto Rican youth in Newark, New Jersey, Ramos-Zayas (2007) observed that one's urbanness was often used to "authenticate" a black identity. The same can be said for the Cape Verdean youth. Many participants pointed out that life is hard in the ghetto. The ghetto in this sense becomes a symbol of authenticity in the conventional sense; it becomes the heart of blackness as identity. Life in the streets of Providence, Brockton, or Dorchester becomes a badge of honor, but also an experience that contributes to racial authenticity and solidarity. A ghetto lifestyle, whether real or imagined, helps connect and forge an imagined community of the oppressed and disavowed; it becomes a tool of mediation. There is a shared sense of identities in struggle. Hegemony and socioeconomic conditions create a setting that cannot help but be valorized by its inhabitants.

David Harvey (1993) notes that place-bound identities are becoming more important, rather than less important. While both federal and state governments have divested in urban areas over the last forty plus years, the Cape Verdean youth I interviewed and observed have overinvested culturally and emotionally in their neighborhoods. In other words, policies of "benign neglect" and structural violence seem to have created a "benign embrace" of dangerous regional localities. As Forman (2002) has shown, to "keep it real" or "represent" in hip-hop is always to represent the hood. This phenomenon in effect has trickled down from hip-hop artists and made its way into the everyday lives of young Cape Verdean men. While I do not doubt the dangerousness of the urban communities my informants are from, I do wonder how much my male informants seized on and exaggerated many of the sensational aspects of urban living, and in doing so neglect the "legacies of normalized racial violence that calcify, but do not guarantee, the denigration of black geographies and their inhabitants" (McKittrick 2011, 950). How much did they exaggerate what civil society and gangsta rappers have been portraying for years? That is, urban violence as a pathological feature of blackness.

It is here where "being urban" can and may support the fantasy life of antiblackness. The ways in which my male informants described their communities tended to reaffirm prejudicial beliefs about predatory inner-city communities and black males. As a result, they reinforced racial stereotypes held by many whites. However, can we blame these youth for perpetuating racial stereotypes? Can we blame them for keeping stereotypes in circulation? As Harvey explains: "Places in the city are dubbed as 'dubious' or 'dangerous,' again leading to patterns of behavior, both public and private, that turn fantasy into reality" (1993, 7). Not only do stereotypes become "common sense," thus reinforcing racial hegemony, but stereotypes also become an existential reality in an antiblack world. Unlike the gangsta rappers who have capitalized on the marketing of the hood or ghetto (Quinn 2004), Cape Verdean youth are unable to exploit "being urban" for capital gain, for not all can become hip-hop artists. Further, exaggerating the dangers of urban locales has a reductive effect, thereby stripping these communities of their sociocultural heterogeneity. In a sense, these communities are far more diverse than their caricatures suggest (Kelley 1997; Jackson 2001).

Sartorial tendencies such as wearing regionally specific athletic paraphernalia (e.g., Boston Red Sox hats) are further illustrative of this point. In other words, "being urban" is protected and authenticated not just through lived experience and spatial residency, but also through "ghetto fabulous" clothing styles associated with hip-hop culture. The ghetto has become a product that is consumed, worn, and embodied.

Most of the informants that I talked with, formally or informally, defined themselves as black. Cape Verdean identities in the Greater Boston area reflect their socialization in low-income urban American environments. Cape Verdean youth grow up in a context (again Hesse's concept of "raceocracy" maybe of some utility) where their skin color, phenotype, geographical location, history, and cultural tendencies, that is, performative practices, mark them as black. Based on these experiences and being structurally positioned as black, Cape Verdeans identify and experience solidarity with groups that they see in the same structural position (with the exception of Latinos). My interviews also suggest that identity is also the result of discourse that is organized by the sociocultural relations of production. In other words, there is a close correlation between race and class relations. They realize that racism can just as easily be aimed at them as at African Americans and other racially marked subjects, that the dominant groups in society seldom differentiate among nonwhite groups giving race a totalizing effect. Many Cape Verdean youth see themselves as black, but this is to be understood as a racial identity and not to be confused with being African American (or black American). Therefore, suggestions that the black/white (nonblack) binary is under radical reconstruction are at best questionable, for the world still remains at its core antiblack.

Intergenerational conflict exists between Cape Verdeans because the two generations have been raised under different social contexts and cultural formations. Cape Verdean youth move away from their parents' generation through corporeal contact and social interaction with other black people. Further, they use a different cultural framework to view themselves, which may highlight that racial identity and racial solidarity in an ever-increasing globalized world are sometimes better predicted by generation *and* corporeality, marking a shift from a politics based on identity to an identity based on politics.

In short, "being black" is not only based on the assemblage and performance of identity, but also organized around power relations and material conditions. Cape Verdean youth are interpellated, called into constructed racial categories, categories that only make sense in a racial hierarchy. To be black in a world where white power is normative is to always be structured in hierarchical relation to that power. The racial self involves thinking of oneself in terms of the prevailing concepts and performative practices of the cultural formations. Although levels of agency are exhibited, these youth exist and act within a set of preexisting assumptions and constraints. Second-generation Cape Verdean youth, racialized as black, are affected by race and actively structure their existence around the reality of its normalizing paradigms while negotiating antagonistic relations to such normalization. Put differently, the Cape Verdean youth I interviewed and observed articulated a dialectical understanding about what blackness means and how it deviates from what they understand as being black.

Kriolu Noize: Bridges of Black Cape Verdean Sound

Within the world of underground hip hop specifically and multiracial American social settings more generally, the idea that race should not matter and the false consciousness (for some) that race does not matter gets consistently confronted by the fact that it does.

—Kwame Anthony Harrison, *Hip Hop Underground*

In January 2006, Cape Verdean hip-hop artist D. Lopes, from Brockton, Massachusetts, performed "My People," a song about Cape Verde and his African roots, for music video show *106 & Park*'s weekly talent show segment "Wild Out Wednesday" on Black Entertainment Television (BET). In one hand D. Lopes held the microphone. In the other hand, he proudly held up the flag of the Republic of Cape Verde. At the conclusion of the show D. Lopes, with a sense of accomplishment having won the talent show, said "I'd like to give a shout out to all Cape Verdeans."

Approximately two years later, on Wednesday, January 6, 2008, I tuned into *106 & Park* to see Cape Verdean hip-hop artist Charles "Chachi" Carvalho. Standing next to host "Roxy," Chachi, from Pawtucket, Rhode Island, outfitted in a beige fedora with a Robert Nesta Marley patch fixed to the side, a black blazer, a green T-shirt with the words "Cabo Verde, Est. 1975" across the front, baggy jeans, and dark colored sneakers, performed "Like I Do" to a screaming crowd. Although not as overt in his pride for Cape Verde as D. Lopes's previous performance on the cable television channel,

Chachi made sure to represent Cape Verde. In fact, he would return to *106 & Park* in the summer to perform "Cape Verdean in America." Both of these moments are significant for two reasons. First, for the Republic of Cape Verde and the diaspora to be represented on cable television was a rare moment. Second, and more importantly, for Cape Verdeans like D. Lopes and Chachi to fit seamlessly on the set of *106 & Park*, a music video show that features popular hip-hop, dancehall, reggae, and contemporary R&B videos, illustrates the ease with which young Cape Verdeans "traffic in blackness" (Elam and Jackson 2005). Their blackness was never questioned. In fact, both D. Lopes and Chachi were successful in winning, by large margins, the popular vote for their respective performances on "Wild Out Wednesdays."

Identities are discursively mediated constructs; that is, we come to understand others and ourselves through discourse. For cultural critic Herman Gray, "Music is about making and remaking subjects and, as such, making and remaking identities" (2005, 153). While scholars have investigated the impact hip-hop culture has on the identities of African American youth (Clay 2003), little has been done on its impact on Africans and African immigrants in particular (Forman 2001; Ibrahim 2014). Therefore, the purpose of this chapter is to map the link between hip-hop culture and Cape Verdean youth subjectivity. This chapter asks the following questions: How does hip-hop inform the lived experiences of Cape Verdean youth? And what do hip-hop texts tell us about these lived experiences? The investment of Cape Verdean youth in black popular culture, particularly hip-hop culture, is not haphazard nor is it by accident. As cultural critic Tricia Rose has pointed out, "We do not invest in cultures randomly; cultural exchanges, desires, appropriations, and affinities always speak to already existing relationships, conscious and otherwise—those we want to reinforce, transform, deny, embrace. . . . The cultural traffic in blackness is part and parcel of a legacy of race" (2005, vii). Thus, what follows is an accounting of the perceived relationship between blackness and hip-hop by the Cape Verdean youth whose experiences grace these pages. Further, I investigate the texts of Cape Verdean hip-hop artists from the Greater Boston area to help define what it means to be young and black in the United States. I will investigate music as a way in which to illustrate how Cape Verdean youth speak about "the lived experience of blackness" and as a way to illustrate blackness as a cultural formation. I attempt to show how music is reflective of social conditions, as well as show how "musical structures intersect with ideological forces to produce and reinforce one another" (James 2005, 178). Race comes into being in part as an accomplishment, which is embedded in the culture industry. As Fanon (1967) observed, culture normalizes the social construction of race.

Hip-hop, which began in the early 1970s in the South Bronx, New York, was no more than a leisurely pursuit developed by disaffected Caribbean, Latino, and African

American youth. Today, hip-hop is a global phenomenon that connects youth across race, income, ethnicity, and geographic boundaries (see Fernandes 2011; Helbig 2014; Ntarangwi 2009; Osumare 2013; Saucier 2011; N. Sharma 2010). In many ways, hip-hop culture today has less to do with a separate and distinct black and Latino perspective and more to do with general youth rebellion and politics. However, race and racial identity, especially blackness, are at the vortex of hip-hop culture; hip-hop is intrinsic to racial identification, and blackness as a social category conveys resistance. More than anything, hip-hop is still seen as the expression of a black racial identity and the collective angst of black (and blackened) youth. Rap music, in particular, remains dominated by black youth in its local, global, and commercial manifestations.

Despite its popularity, hip-hop is a space, at times, of resistance, of marking the general antagonism that is blackness. Today, many hip-hop artists, although not all, see themselves as artists and activists, fusing the various elements of hip-hop culture with politics (see Clay 2012; Kitwana 2014; Watkins 2005). Beyond protest lyrics, hip-hop has also developed vibrant organizations and political platforms that have enhanced its activist edge, known as hip-hop activism. For instance, hip-hop was central to many of the youth workshops of the World Conference against Racism and Xenophobia in Durban, South Africa, and has made its way into the movement for national and international reparations for colonialism and slavery among many other things. Due to the emergence of various organizations and activist networks, hip-hop culture has both a national and international political agenda that reflects current socioeconomic and political tensions.

Despite being filled with contradictions and commercial visibility, hip-hop is more than music. It is a cultural formation that articulates youth estrangement, economic hardship, political disenfranchisement, and more generally social death. Although hip-hop culture has issues with heteropatriarchy and commercial cooptation—the fruits of living in an antiblack world—it also provides a space to advocate for social justice and freedom among disaffected blackened youth, a space to stitch together the fragments of dispossession. Hip-hop is a collection of forms and practices that helps its practitioners and consumers to better map the culture of politics (see Asante 2009; Clay 2012; Rabaka 2013).

Hip-Hop and Cape Verdean Youth

Embracing blackness and expressing a degree of urban competency is insufficient or inadequate for second-generation Cape Verdean youth. Racial belonging needs to be followed by the production and consumption of culture. Despite the multiple sites where blackness is constructed, hip-hop culture takes precedence over other sites. As Andreana Clay (2003, 2012), Murray Forman (2001), and others have observed, youth perform hip-hop culture as a primary racial signifier for blackness. Hip-hop's performative practices are used at times to "authenticate" a conventional black identity that instrumentalizes the repression of blackness, but they also illustrate a level of racial sincerity, an intent and proactive investment and engagement in being black.

For the majority of Cape Verdean youth, "being black" includes adopting a hip-hop style. The clothing is hip-hop inspired. The English they speak is inflected with hip-hop terms and verbal stylizations. The fact that most of my informants have adopted a hip-hop style contributes to their "being black" and it illustrates their embrace of a thick conception of blackness; that is, blackness is not only biologically defined, but also a cultural formation.

My interest in the connection between hip-hop and the performance of race stems not only from my interest in hip-hop culture in general, but also, and more importantly, from the obvious centrality of hip-hop in popular culture in the lives of youth locally and globally. Similar to Somalian teens in North America, Cape Verdean youth in the Greater Boston area "encounter the hegemonic authority of the hip-hop culture" (Forman 2001, 50).[1] As Murray Forman argues "'real' black identities are given voice in complex and often vitriolic terms in hip hop" (2001, 51). In addition, Paul Gilroy has claimed that hip-hop is "the very blackest of culture—one that provides the scale on which all others can be evaluated" (quoted in Clay 2003, 1348). If Cape Verdean youth are racialized as black and hip-hop is the blackest culture to date, it is useful to determine the significance of hip-hop for Cape Verdean identity. The adoption of hip-hop indexes the shift in Cape Verdean identity from the past to the present. Rather than disassociate themselves with something labeled "black," as previous generations had, many of my informants embrace hip-hop for its perceived blackness. Many of the Cape Verdean youth that I encountered use hip-hop as a form of cultural capital in everyday settings, which in turn authenticates an essentialized black identity and illustrates blackness as a political commitment.

PKS: Is there anything that ties hip-hop with being Cape Verdean?

JUVENAL: Being black! The funny thing is the newer generation is more accepting of being defined as black. We live in the same neighborhoods. We go through the same things. . . . Cape Verdeans don't realize they're black until they run into the cops. If they have any legal troubles, they're going to get treated the same way. So what if you have a Portuguese last name. They look at your skin complexion and it's a rap for you. That's when Cape Verdeans realize, yo' we're really black. . . . As Cape Verdeans we're always identified as black no matter how light skinned we are. If you're at a white friend's house and something goes missing, their parents will be like that black kid did it.

Hip-hop is black. Although it's open to everybody, this is our music. It's black music. It's black style. The thing about hip-hop and being black is it almost seems as if you're supposed to like it. People don't even question if you really like hip-hop, they just assume. Being black is enough. Being black and listening to hip-hop is authentic enough. People don't question you.

Luis states, "I first became interested in hip-hop after watching music videos on BET and MTV. I could relate to them; we black people." He went on to say that he first identified with hip-hop because of the skin color of most hip-hop artists and believes it would have been difficult to relate to hip-hop if the artists were predominately white. For Luis, the social commentary was secondary but no less important than skin color and phenotype. "Hip-hop," he stated, "shows you that we all go through the same shit. People don't understand things are hard and difficult." Luis continued, "Hip-hop reflects my background. How the world *is*. What 50 Cent and Lil Wayne talk about speaks to me because it's hard out there and they know what it's like to be a black man." Put simply, hip-hop often reflects the lived experience of blackness. Similarly, Antonio, a twenty-one-year-old from Providence, had this to say about hip-hop and being black.

PKS: Why hip-hop? What is it about hip-hop that makes you want to listen to the music and be part of its culture?

ANTONIO: It reflects me, my mind state as a black man in the United States. The artists talk directly to me. The experiences they talk about resonate with me and my life. Hip-hop parallels my life. It's connected to growing up poor in South Providence. Mobb Deep, for instance, reflects my mind state.

PKS: Anything else? What else draws you to hip-hop as a culture?

ANTONIO: I mean hip-hop is black. Hip-hop wouldn't speak to me if it was about middle-class white America. Black people are pushed into the same areas, regardless of our differences, and hip-hop gets that.

PKS: Do you do anything else besides listen to hip-hop music?

ANTONIO: I'm a product of hip-hop. Most of what I do is because of hip-hop. The way I dress, speak, even walk is because of hip-hop. The way I shake hands. The way I greet people. Hip-hop influences everything I do.

In her commentary on hip-hop, blackness, and identity, Carmen from Brockton, spoke more about the cultural origins of hip-hop and its relation to her "being black" as reasons for her interest and love for hip-hop. As she stated, "Hip-hop derives from Africa. So that's why I feel I assimilate better with hip-hop. The roots of hip-hop are African, and since I'm African, its roots match mine." The adoption of hip-hop culture by many of my informants is a way to cultivate a thick conception of black subjectivity. For many of my informants, physical appearance is not enough, but it should never be left out. Acknowledgment of one's African ancestry or Africanity is also not enough. Thus, a thick black identity is assumed through hip-hop's performative practices. This highlights being black is not just a matter of common physical appearance and shared ancestry, but a matter of common cultural practices. Racial identity and culture become linked and indistinguishable. For instance, Carmen emphasized the fact that hip-hop is African in origin or at the very least traceable to the culture of African ancestors, thus making her participation in the culture almost automatic and predetermined. Others stressed the connection between the experiences of black people with oppression and the rich culture they have created out of that context.

Partaking in hip-hop culture via its production and/or consumption contributes to the racializing of second-generation Cape Verdean youth in the Greater Boston area. There was a sense among many of my informants that since hip-hop is viewed as black culture par excellence or African in its origin they must enjoy some aspects of its culture and participate in some of its performative practices. To *be* black and not participate in hip-hop culture are grounds for questioning one's racial subjectivity. Thus, to embrace hip-hop illustrates a level of intent and sincerity about being black in the United States. One is not black, at least in the thick sense of blackness, unless one has embraced the culture of hip-hop.

CAPE VERDEAN NOIZE

Hip-hop culture and rap lyrics, in particular, help define what it means to be young and black in the United States. Since Cape Verdean youth are primarily consumers of hip-hop culture, and as a result are influenced by both the local and global presence of hip-hop, I offer the following investigation into the lyrics of some Cape Verdean hip-hop artists, namely Chachi Carvalho, D. Lopes, and Tem Blessed. I chose these artists largely due to their popularity among second-generation Cape Verdean youth in the Greater Boston area. Hip-hop music performed by Cape Verdean artists is instructive, for it allows for us to "examine the contexts and processes that produce the narratives commonly found in rap music" (Neal 1997, 134). In other words, what does the music tell us about being Cape Verdean in America?

Too often the idea of indigenization, the reformulation of cultures within sets of specific localisms, is applied to the study of foreign societies and cultures, and not to local cultural communities. Like other cultural forms, hip-hop in the Cape Verdean diaspora, particularly in New England, has been localized and indigenized in relation to the political, economic, and sociocultural realities of Cape Verdean youth. Hip-hop speaks to the reality of Cape Verdeans in the United States, past and present. More robustly, it speaks of their encounters with antiblackness.

Both Chachi and D. Lopes tackle the experience of Cape Verdeans in the United States with songs like "Cape Verdean in America" and "My People." In "My People" D. Lopes speaks not of his struggles in the United States, but of his mother's struggles related to being a first-generation immigrant and a women raising kids in a land with little opportunity for those racialized as black. Similarly, Chachi's "Cape Verdean in America" speaks candidly of the struggles many Cape Verdean youth experience, the reason why the song was a major success on the New England hip-hop scene. As one informant enthusiastically said to me, "Everything you hear in that song, I've been through. I've *lived.*"

In "Cape Verdean in America," Chachi not only illustrates for its listeners what Cape Verdeans endure in the United States, he simultaneously uncovers and deconstructs the idea that America is the land of opportunity and freedom. Chachi begins his narrative by racializing the subject:

Yo', light-skin, African-blood
Born in America
The land of the slave with a raft and flood
Where they're quick to leave your ass in a tub
With no water to drink and grub
So we trapped in the mud
Growin' up pockets were broke
Kicks were trashed
So if I couldn't crack back
I just kicked some ass.

A catchy, yet descriptive and disheartening, chorus line then follows the first verse:

Do you know what it's like?
To be a Cape Verdean in America
You gotta know how to fight
Cuz' the world's so cold in America

And they cut off ya' heat and lights
If you can't pay your bills in America
And you know that ain't right
Yup, no, no, no!

In verse two, Chachi explains his efforts not to be confused with an immigrant, while also telling Cape Verdeans who desire to come to America that it is not exactly the land of opportunity, rather the land of low-wage employment and soullessness. In Marxian style, Chachi briefly alludes to the fetishization of commodities and by extension alienation. Chachi's constant referencing of America, I believe, is evidence that he sees alienation as an individual condition, but also a structural concept. Chachi is keenly aware of patterns of individual competitive materialism and the exploitative relationship between capital and labor, and wishes to bestow this knowledge on the listener. Chachi writes:

Growin' up in Pawtucket had to roll wit' a team
Down to fight anybody tryin' to call you a green
All guts, no glory when you young on the scene
When my cousin learned English his swagger was mean
U.S. is like a different world
Cuz my cousin couldn't speak no English
Still get all the girls
Flavaless flavor
TVs, DVDs, CDs, got all that
America ain't what it seems to be
You lose soul, like fingers, in machinery
Or sweepin' floors up in Newport Creamery
And everybody's mama made jewelry.

Rap music is also used to discuss other issues like violence and deportation, issues both real and dear to the Cape Verdean community in the Greater Boston area. Hip-hop not only describes the realties confronting Cape Verdean youth, it also provides an outlet for coping with said realities. In several songs on his album *The Challenge, Mixtape, Vol. 2*, Tem Blessed, a Cape Verdean rapper from New Bedford, Massachusetts, articulates a high degree of concern for the violence plaguing black communities. With a slow, methodical, almost depressing beat, Tem Blessed in "4 Black Males Die" tells his listeners about the ubiquity of death plaguing black males throughout the world. In "Too Much Blood" he regrettably informs the listener:

So much killing around me
It's astounding to see
So much death in this black community
Losing three homeboys in a month, not uncommon
Foolishly, they increase the police ta' keep bombin'.

In "Welcome to Bedrock" Tem explores the violent conditions of his hometown of New Bedford. At the time of my research, according to the FBI's annual Uniform Crime Report for 2006, New Bedford had the fourth most reports of violent crimes in Massachusetts. D. Lopes from Brockton, rapping about the life and work of Amílcar Cabral, concludes his tribute to Cabral by stating, "He did everything . . . So that we could live in this world. Now we out here killing each other."[2] This final statement is one of urgency and a direct reference to the gratuitous violence occurring in Brockton, violence that has touched the life of D. Lopes and other Cape Verdean youth in the area.

Chachi and D. Lopes also mention deportation in their lyrical passages. The Illegal Immigration Reform and Immigrant Responsibility Act of 1996 permitted the deportation of immigrants nationwide convicted of crimes and undocumented status. As a result, deportation became automatic, regardless of the circumstances of the crime, how long the immigrant had been in the United States, or whether they had reformed since committing the crime. Since 1996 nearly one thousand Cape Verdeans have been deported from the United States, with the overwhelming majority due to criminal activity, not undocumented status (U.S. Department of Justice, Immigration and Naturalization Service 1999; U.S. Department of Homeland Security, Office of Immigration Statistics 2005). The deportation of Cape Verdean youth from the Greater Boston area to Cape Verde has sparked controversy from within the Cape Verdean community, much of which is concerned with the so-called nihilistic nature of committing urban crimes, all of which stinks of moralistic authority and paternalism in the service of civil society. Deportation, I would argue, is just another mechanism of (re)racialization through the intensification of antiblackness.

Given the harsh realities of daily life, the violence, incarceration, poverty, and deportation, in their lyrics and in conversation with me many Cape Verdean artists evoked the ideas of repatriation, a return to the motherland, namely Cape Verde. Both D. Lopes and Chachi speak nostalgically of a return to Cape Verde. D. Lopes urges all Cape Verdeans to return at some point in their life, for it will bring clarity to one's identity and position in life. Despite having never visited Cape Verde at the time of the interview, Chachi sees the archipelago as his future home.[3] As he stated one night, "I see myself returning to Cape Verde, although I've never been, for the American dream is clearly a myth. It does not include black people. There is little room for minorities."

To this end, the islands are viewed not as an accessible holiday where one simply attends clubs, eats *cachupa*, and visits relatives. Instead, the islands are the ideal backdrop to experiment with ideas of liberation, freedom, and hope. Rap not only allows for the illustration of nostalgic images of the archipelago; it allows Cape Verdean youth to celebrate, preserve, and extend what is uniquely Cape Verdean, namely the political message of national liberation of Amílcar Cabral.

POLITICAL ACTIVISM, LEADERSHIP, AND HIP-HOP CULTURE

The politics and black consciousness of the 1960s and 1970s continue to live on via the musical and poetic talents of hip-hop artists. Conscious rap, as it is known, exerts a powerful political influence on its youthful listeners. Hip-hop, as already mentioned, has become a major vehicle for disenfranchised youth to express their worldview, concerns, and dreams. Conscious rap speaks with a sense of urgency, emerging out of economic depravity, psychological enslavement, and political trickery, while also building on the rich tradition of black poets such as June Jordan, Gil-Scott Heron, Amiri Baraka, and the Last Poets, to name a few.

Throughout the album *The Challenge, Mixtape, Vol. 2* Tem Blessed plays with popular and commercialized rap songs. Often keeping the beats and melodies of the originals, Tem Blessed changes the lyrical content of these songs, removing the misogyny and destructive behavior for a politics of freedom and justice. In other words, he takes on the practice of signifyin(g), a rhetorical device used to apply new meanings to old symbols and ideas (see Potter 1995). In describing the art of sampling, a means of signifyin(g), music scholar Joseph Schloss argues, "it allows individuals to demonstrate intellectual power while simultaneously obscuring the nature and extent of their agency. . . . It allows producers to *use other people's music to convey their own compositional ideas*" (2004, 138, emphasis added).

Rather than have continuing dreams of commercial success and intercourse with R&B singers, like commercial rapper The Game envisioned in his popular music single "Dreams,"[4] Tem Blessed signifies on the hypnotic beat of the original in his song "Dream," and with a stroke of honesty, self-introspection, and determination states:

> I too had dreams of fucking R&B chicks
> Now my dream consists of feeding the kids
> This world is sick
> Packed in like project bricks

Just trying to live like Africans on slave ships
Think, list of dreams
Platinum and diamond scenes
My black brothers and sisters living like kings and queens
Gold mines and mountain springs mold minds to climb high.

This freedom dream, according to Tem Blessed, will be the result of praxis, that is, the actions of a "Black Panther super soldier destroyin' this bitch ass system." Similarly, Tem signifies on Southern rapper David Banner's hit single "Play."[5] Banner's original song is bawdy and course, as the chorus illustrates:

Cum girl, I'm tryna get your pussy wet
Work that, lemme see you drip sweat
Cum girl, I'm tryna get your pussy wet
Work that, lemme see you drip sweat
Gon play with it
Gon play with it
Gon play with it
Gon play with it
Gon play with it
Work that clit
Cum girl.

Following this raunchy and explicit chorus, David Banner continues to take the listener on a verbal sexual escapade, filled with oral sex, female objectification, and sexual domination. In an ironic twist, with the catchy head-nodding beat of the original, Tem Blessed gives the listener "Run Girl," which articulates the rapper's enthusiasm for the impending revolution, leaving out the heteropatriarchy of the popular David Banner original. The chorus of "Run Girl" is as follows:

Run girl, tell someone the revolution has just begun
Run girl, tell someone the revolution has just begun
Run girl, tell someone the revolution has just begun
Run girl, tell someone the revolution has just begun.

Following the chorus, Tem Blessed tells the listener about building progressive social institutions for "the people," institutions prefaced on the ideas of Malcolm X and Huey P. Newton. Given that the CD is a mixtape, "Run Girl" seamlessly blends into the next track "Lace them Boots," which builds on the ideas and practices explicated in "Run Girl." Only this time, Tem Blessed does not use a popular commercial beat and signify on its content. Instead, he uses an original beat and employs the poetics of Umar Bin Hassan of the Last Poets, a group of poets and musicians from the late 1960s and early 1970s inspired by black nationalism and the politics of the Black Power movement. Umar's presence on the track gives the song's idea of "people power" and revolution historical continuity with the past. His poetics serve as a bridge between generations confronting similar social problems. Umar recapitulates Tem's call that the revolution has not been completed, that the fight for freedom must continue if people, black people, are to achieve full human potential and dignity.

Despite his deep desire for a social revolution, never for a moment does Tem Blessed give the listener the idea that social justice will simply be given or that revolution will be easy. In fact, as the title track alludes, it will be a challenge. Thus, what is in order is a "return to the source," a reference to a volume containing some of the principal speeches Amílcar Cabral delivered in his last years during visits to the United States. More generally, Tem's call is to access the words and wisdom of past freedom fighters like Cabral and Malcolm X in order to provide guidance for the fight for justice in the new millennium. Through his music, he urges Cape Verdean and black youth alike to identify closely with the historic and contemporary struggles and learn from their positive and negative experiences. As Chachi expresses in the last verse of "Cape Verdean in America":

And this is for Amílcar Cabral
Who taught us all how to love
But sometimes we got ta' throw on gloves
And we still need him
We still fightin' for freedom.

As Homi Bhabha has observed, "remembering is never a quiet act of introspection or retrospection. It is a painful re-membering, a putting together of the dismembered past to make sense of the trauma of the present" (1986, xxiii). The referencing of Cabralian politics and use of black national sentiments (and black nationalists like Umar Bin Hassan) illustrates a bridging and intersecting of Cape Verdean and African American identities, showing similarities in the black experience and by extension the black condition. It creates the potential to forge a radical politics, a politics of identification prefaced on the experiences and historical affinities of black people globally (see Vargas 2008). To this end, hip-hop is a space where Cape Verdean youth can and do use identity as a site of sociopolitical struggle to strategically forge their imagined communities. The racialization of Cape Verdean youth also serves as an impetus for political mobilization. Similar to Amílcar Cabral, Tem Blessed, Chachi, and others stand for peace and justice. Their lyrics confront invisible forms of oppression and the dehumanizing racial violence of the U.S. and global economy. As Peter McLaren argues, "rap urges the creation of cooperatives of resistance, zones of freedom, where strategies and tactics of liberation can emerge" (1997, 176).[6] This may be easier to accomplish not only because hip-hop is a space for "reasoned comparison," but also because it has emotive qualities.

Although the experience of being black offers a potential for coalition building in the name of blackness and community, we must also be wary of the impact and social force of hip-hop, for music in itself is not politically transgressive; to offer a critique of the material-social relations of exploitation is not enough. Music only becomes transgressive when it is inscribed in the actions and activities of people and groups. Despite their commercial success, albeit on a local and regional level, the importance of building real social institutions has not been lost in the lyrical finesse of Cape Verdean rappers like Chachi and Tem Blessed. Both, along with other Cape Verdean artists, have been central in establishing and participating in grassroots organizations in the Greater Boston area. Hip-hop has in many respects filled the void of not having a large mass-based social movement. For instance, Chachi has founded Beat Box Studios, a place where aspiring artists can record and learn about the art of rapping and turntableism, and is the creator of the now defunct Peace Fest. According to a flyer distributed during the fourth annual Rhode Island Hip Hop Peace Fest (2007):

Peace Fest was an idea created to raise awareness about the dangers of gun violence in our music and in our communities and how it affects our everyday lives. By combing the visual arts community, local media and the local community of musicians we would be spreading the message through the voices that create change and really make a difference. Everyone involved has their own story to tell . . . we will not stand aside and watch violence ruin our neighborhoods and poison our youth. We celebrate life through music and shed positive light on hip hop as a culture. . . . *The goal of this event is to enlighten, enrich, educate and motivate all those involved to join us in the continuous struggle to stop senseless violence and encourage those around us to spread a little love.* (emphasis added)

Tem Blessed has been affiliated with 3rd Eye Unlimited of New Bedford, a non-profit youth organization. Third Eye's vision is to

1. Build a movement to improve the community, centered around the principles of economic and social equality, with young people being an integral part of that movement in roles of leadership and action.

2. Empower youth to think critically and independently, therefore fostering a heightened understanding of themselves, their peers, and important societal issues.

3. Build leadership skills by providing valuable experience in organizing, video production, event planning, and community outreach.

4. Create positive activities for inner city youth that aim to promote their talents and bring people together in a safe, energetic atmosphere.

5. Raise awareness in our community by advancing the positive and progressive aspects of the Hip Hop culture, which challenges the social status quo, and offers an array of diverse and unique ideas to society. We strive to give young people a chance for their ideas to be developed and their voices to be heard, regardless of race, creed, or religion.

6. Provide forums that allow young people to express themselves, to communicate with other youth, and to create art that is reflective of themselves and their environment.[7]

Not all Cape Verdean artists are engaged in progressive politics. Some fall victim to the (anti)black popular culture forms in circulation. While D. Lopes attempts to communicate a level of social consciousness, he also attempts to capture the themes, idioms, and iconography of the pimp and the playa, as do other Cape Verdean artists. To this end, white supremacy and antiblackness have become so hegemonic that they have even annexed and colonized the blackest of cultural forms, hip-hop. Thus, hip-hop as a site of resistance is put into question—the very means by which some youth asserted their humanity is limiting. As Andrea Queeley has observed, "Black performers have always been pressured to perform the Blackness of the white imagination, and that Blackness is most often in the service of white supremacy" (2003, 4). Further she states, hip-hop helps to reinforce "the naturalization of black criminality that is deeply rooted in the ideology and economy of the United States" (9). Looking at and listening to Cape Verdean youth hip-hop, one is struck by its duality, its two faces: those of voyeuristic spectacle and of community creation. This antagonism can also be read as the antagonism in identity that emerges from their narratives.

As empirical evidence shows, hip-hop culture is important and has special meaning for Cape Verdean youth. It allows Cape Verdeans to celebrate their Cape Verdean heritage while absorbing and producing black cultural markers. Simultaneously, hip-hop is used to identify with the struggle of "being black." Hip-hop for artists like Tem Blessed is political and empowering, for hip-hop provides a space to give voice to their struggles, their lived experience with antiblackness. Hip-hop is a way to link struggles across borders, to create "bridges of sound"; hip-hop allows for the framing of black history and political struggle (Cooper 2004). Cape Verdean youth privilege hip-hop as a site for political information about their racialized selves. In other words, young Cape Verdeans are turning to hip-hop and other forms of popular culture in lieu of narratives available in traditional institutions. As radical geographer Michel de Certeau (1984) has observed, popular culture is a resource used to make sense of the world. In the end, being black and young in the twenty-first century is intrinsically related to hip-hop culture. Hip-hop culture and the lyrical content of rap music indexes a shift in the racial identification of Cape Verdean youth in the Greater Boston area.

Cape Verdean Youth Cool: Tailoring Identity

Several hundred festival attendees are standing, sitting, and roaming within the festival confines, an erected makeshift fence. Over twenty clothing and food vendors are participating in the Providence Cape Verdean Independence Festival, creating a cacophony of sound, smell, and color. The smell of grilled food (charred chicken in particular) is thick, with hints of *cachupa* and fresh coconut. Traditional and modern forms of Cape Verdean music are piped through the large speakers at decibel levels high enough to disrupt conversations taking place between festival goers. Old and new Cape Verdean flags are everywhere. Both are being flown above vendor tents and tables. They are being sold, either as flags or imprinted on shirts. As the attendees make their way through the sea of vendors, young Cape Verdean men wear baseball caps twisted to the side. Many are draped in the green, red, and gold of the old Cape Verdean flag; the flag is being used as a head-wrap, as a bag, for shorts, and it is imprinted on T-shirts. . . . Aside from flags being worn on the body, the latest in hip-hop fashion is exhibited. Young Cape Verdean men are wearing oversized basketball jerseys, ultravoluminous jean shorts, and big sunglasses. Many have their hair braided (i.e., in cornrows). Some are sporting fads. Of the clothing name brands I can visibly identify, all are popular within hip-hop, such as LRG, Rocawear, Saucony, Eckō Unltd., etc. Platinum and silver jewelry is popular, particularly long necklaces with crosses. . . . Tattoos are also prominently displayed on the arms of many Cape Verdean youth.

—Field notes, Greater Boston area

Initially, questions of fashion and style were simply going to play a peripheral role in my portrayal of Cape Verdean blackness. However, after I attended many events, the importance of fashion and style became increasingly noticeable. Looking over my field notes from festivals, like the one described above, and various other cultural events (e.g., music concerts and college student group events), I was struck by how much space I dedicated to describing what people were wearing, how they were wearing their clothes, the colors and size of their clothes, and the name brands the wearer fancied. The clothing, hairstyles, jewelry, sneakers, and tattoos of Cape Verdean youth had a communicative quality to them in that the sartorial tastes of my informants and those observed from afar said something to me. They communicated to me who they were, or at the very least who they wanted you to think they were. From this, I began to realize the centrality of the clothed and decorated body in constructing and maintaining an identity, particularly a racial (and ethnic) identity. In other words, clothing styles are more than trends and must always be understood in relation to the larger social context and cultural politics that are being articulated through them. Clothing is one way, of many, for people to assemble political and racial subjectivities. Clothing, in this sense, rather that illustrating a text actually textualizes space (racialized space). Consequently, fashion is never innocent and is more than mere appearance (Barnard 2002).

The body as a social canvas has been called "the symbolic stage upon which the drama of socialization is enacted" (Turner 1980, 112). The body adorned with its clothing and other sartorial accoutrements has semiotic value and social import. Using participant observation and textual analysis, this chapter investigates popular, political, and economic meanings assigned to treatments of the body. I look at the ways in which Cape Verdean youth in the Greater Boston area assemble individual and social identities via fashion. This chapter highlights a semiotic web and performative practices where local, national, and global identities are negotiated, constructed, and assembled. To this end, this chapter asks a series of questions about the commitments brought to notice by clothes and fashion. First, how important is fashion in the creation and maintenance of identity? Second, how does the powerful and hegemonic racial coding of clothes and style affect the use of clothing by Cape Verdean youth? Last, what do the clothes Cape Verdean youth wear say about who they are *and* what they are?

After briefly looking at fashion as a form of communication and hip-hop fashion, I turn my attention to the sartorial practices of Cape Verdean youth. I look specifically at the wearing of the Cape Verdean flag and images of Amílcar Cabral on T-shirts. I then turn my attention to the intersections between fashion and masculinity and the economic space Cape Verdean fashion has created for Cape Verdean entrepreneurs.

FASHION AS COMMUNICATION

Fashion is a primary symbol in the construction and reconstruction of multiple subjectivities. It implies a move away from clothing as necessity, to clothing as a display
of identity. Fashion is dynamic in that it allows individuals to express individual and
group difference, while also allowing conformity with a group. In other words, fashion
is an intensely personal phenomenon since it creates difference, yet, simultaneously,
it is an important social phenomenon in that it creates solidarity; it allows personal
values to be expressed at the same time norms are followed (Simmel 1904). For instance, wearing a National Basketball Association (NBA) authentic basketball jersey
conforms to a current fashion trend within hip-hop culture. Yet wearing an NBA jersey
specific to the wearer's hometown and with one's last name imprinted on the back,
as opposed to the last name of a real NBA player, creates a level of distinction among
those who wear NBA jerseys within hip-hop culture.

Fashion is a form of nonverbal communication. The dressed body communicates
our personal and social identities (see Barnard 2002; Barthes 1967; Calefato 2004;
Damhorst et al. 2005; Lurie 2000). It expresses our thoughts, feelings, and desires,
as well as group belonging (Hebdige 1979). Fashion is revealing, in that it separates
people into groups—black, white, rich, poor, hip-hop, goth, prep, to name a few.
Sartorial practices become signs that say something about the wearers, allowing the
wearers to communicate with their clothes. As anthropologist Hildi Hendrickson has
observed "the body surface is an especially compelling indexical sign. Bodily signifiers
present an ever-present semiotic possibility for expressing identity and intention, for
asserting the legitimacy of the status quo or subverting it" (1996, 14–15). One way
to attempt to subvert the racial status quo is to challenge the conventional uses and
spaces of clothing, to recontextualize them (see Allman 2004; Gott and Loughran
2010; Hebdige 1979). For instance, young Cape Verdeans may wear army fatigues and
Timberland boots, known as "Tims," to "make clear the severity of the urban storms to
be weathered" (Rose 1994, 38). In this case, fatigues and boots are still used for war,
but not a war fought overseas, rather one fought daily in urban and antiblack settings
throughout the United States.

Further, the meanings a person attributes to clothing and fashion are based on
his or her socialization within a particular historical and cultural context (Hebdige
1979). In other words, fashion is context dependent. If we go back to the NBA jersey,
we can see that the jersey worn by an NBA player on the basketball court conveys the
occupational identity of the wearer, while an NBA jersey on the shoulders of someone

in the arena who stands watching a live basketball performance communicates the wearer is a fan, and quite possibly a fan of a particular player.

In short, fashion and clothing constitute signifying systems in which a social order is constructed and communicated (Barthes 1967). High-end acquisitions such as Armani suits and Salvatore Ferragamo shoes might communicate to the observer that the wearer is upper class, while clothes from Walmart might communicate the opposite, that the wearer is working-class or poor.[1] For the purposes of this book, what is important is that the racial structuring of a society often calls forth expressions of race (and ethnicity) via fashion. Racialized subjectivities often demand one dress in a particular way; markers such as skin color and phenotype are not enough in authenticating one's racial identity. Similar to gender, race and ethnicity as social performances involve the adoption of certain accessories and style of dress in order to accomplish race (see Butler 1999; Garfinkel 1967). Falling back on the notion that hip-hop is the blackest of cultures, to be young and black is to dress within the confines of hip-hop culture. In doing so, one establishes a form of blackness. Fashion becomes significant because it communicates who is and who isn't authentic and sincere.

HIP-HOP FASHION

Over the centuries, fashion has been one of the ways in which people of the African diaspora have created their sense of self, sense of community, and sense of place. Bodily practices have been almost as important as political manifestos in the struggle for freedom, agency, and identity. Often political ideologies are accompanied by sartorial practices. Thus, there is an added importance to the ways in which black people in diaspora have dressed and adorned themselves. For example, black cultural nationalism promoted by Mulana Karenga and other cultural nationalists of the 1960s and 1970s advocated for natural hairstyles (e.g., the Afro) and African-styled clothing, such as the dashiki. In many ways, members of the Black Panther Party for Self-Defense are known more for wearing black leather coats and black berets than for their political radicalism. Today, hip-hop fashion is an extension of the ways in which blackness as an identity is conveyed. To be black and young is to dress in accordance with the sartorial ethos of hip-hop culture.

Hip-hop fashion partly expresses the ideas and attitudes of hip-hop culture. Hip-hop style is, and has been for nearly forty years, an extension of black style and fashion. It is a style that has appropriated and experimented with other taste cultures. In the 1980s, hip-hop fashion included sportswear brands such as Le Coq Sportif and Adidas. Clark shoes, namely Wallabees, and Adidas shelltoe sneakers were the footwear of choice, while popular accessories included Kangol bucket hats and heavy gold jewelry. In the late 1980s and early 1990s, "African cool" replaced the sartorial practices of the early 1980s. Hip-hop artists drew from the black cultural nationalism of the 1960s and 1970s and appeared in videos and concerts wearing African jewelry and clothing. Along with African cool, "gangsta" styles emerged on the West coast. Central to the "gangsta" style were Dickies pants, white T-shirts, and black Los Angeles Raiders Starter jackets and baseball caps. In the mid-1990s, baggy clothing became the norm. Members of the hip-hop community wore ultravoluminous shirts, athletic jerseys, and pants. Platinum jewelry also replaced gold as the metal of choice in hip-hop fashion. Today, the baggy style remains, as does diamond-encrusted platinum jewelry. However, recent developments in hip-hop fashion include the reemergence of the styles of the 1980s and African cool. It is possible to attribute the renewed interest in African fashion and style to the increase in African immigrants to the United States. It can also be attributed to the popularity of Jamhuri Wear, a brand from Tanzania popularized by Jay-Z, as well as to the rise of Senegalese hip-hop artist Akon and his Konvict Clothing line. Also, in the late 1990s, hip-hop fashion labels emerged. Notable labels included LRG, Enyce, FUBU, Phat Farm, Baby Phat, Eckō Unltd., and others. In the end, hip-hop fashion is about mixing street fashion with high fashion. It is about excess and style. As Rose suggests, the "exceptionally large gold and diamond jewelry (usually fake) mocks, yet affirms the gold fetish in Western trade . . . [while] Gucci and other designer emblems cut-up and patch-stitched to jackets, pants, hats, wallets, and sneakers in custom shops, work as a form of sartorial warfare" (1994, 37–38). Whether it is chunk gold jewelry or $500 retro Nike Air Force Ones, excess has always been part of hip-hop fashion and can be read as a means of transcending, momentarily, the limitations of life and racial and class positions.

Regardless of time period, as sociologists Robin Chandler and Nuri Chandler-Smith have observed, "Hip-hop folks (hip-hop heads) are defined by their gear" (2005, 231). Style is of the utmost importance to creating and sustaining a subcultural identity. Like fashion in general, hip-hop fashion has its own structure. Youth never "just dress," but "wear" within a set of norms and forms that are considered appropriate (Barthes 1967). Wearing within the fashion structure of hip-hop is as much about what one wears as how one wears it, that is, how one stylizes their clothing and accessories.

Throughout the years the shades and shapes of hip-hop fashion have changed; there exists an ongoing redefinition of what it means to be hip-hop, and by extension what it means to be black, through how the body is dressed. Black youth are always looking for ways to subvert mainstream clothing. Yet hip-hop fashion has become mainstream; it is a prominent part of popular fashion and the cultural barometer for what is cool and hip among youth globally. Today, hip-hop fashion defines the look of global youth culture, which includes boutique clothing, baggy designer jeans, expensive athletic apparel (e.g., professional basketball and football jerseys), fitted baseball caps, sneakers (both retro and new styles), tracksuits, and goose-down winter coats. A quick glance at *Complex* magazine, *The Source*, *XXL*, and other media outlets such as music videos and Instagram photos immediately gives one an idea of the overall, and current, fashion system of hip-hop. In the end, the highly distinctive and ever-changing styles created by black youth of the African diaspora have been influenced by the desire to forge a distinct identity and strengthen group solidarity.

THE SARTORIAL PRACTICES OF CAPE VERDEAN YOUTH

The sartorial practices of Cape Verdean youth in the Greater Boston area illustrate the importance of fashion in the ongoing process of assembling subjectivities. It has become clear through countless hours of formal and informal observation that fashion allows for the drawing of boundaries and construction of narratives of being/becoming/belonging. Cape Verdean youths' emphasis on their blackness in interviews as well as their interest in hip-hop music is matched by the clothing worn and body adornments they fancy. Through these performative practices they are performing race, more specifically blackness. They are authenticating twenty-first-century Cape Verdean blackness. To be young, black, and Cape Verdean in the Greater Boston area is to dress within a specifically defined fashion system influenced by hip-hop culture.

The first time I met eighteen-year-old Juvenal, with his milk-chocolate skin tone and low-cut Caesar fade, he was wearing baggy Mecca blue jeans, a large stylish aqua-blue Polo shirt, and white-and-aqua-blue Nike Air Force Ones. The next time I saw Juvenal his style had changed little, only this time the aqua blue and white were replaced with black and gray. As I continued to see him at music concerts and cultural festivals, he continued to wear baggy pants and loose shirts. His sneakers always matched his shirt. Similarly, Luis, with his light coffee–colored skin and cornrows, was consistently wearing baggy jeans, ultravoluminous T-shirts, and platinum jewelry. The clothing labels he fancied were always graphically imprinted on the front or back of his T-shirts. Labels included LRG, Konvict Clothing, G-Unit, to name a few. Other informants, like twenty-one-year-old Soraya, used hip-hop fashion in her effort to adorn her body, despite disliking the music and other aspects of the culture. For instance, when I first met Soraya she was wearing studded Apple Bottoms capri pants, a gold-colored studded Apple Bottoms tube top, and matching gold pumps.

Weeks later, Soraya was wearing light brown Baby Phat Bermuda shorts, low-top white and pink Nike Air Force Ones, and a pink Baby Phat scoop-neck T-shirt. It was clear that hip-hop fashion had an influence on the sartorial practices of Cape Verdean youth.

Similar to uniforms and dress codes, the hip-hop outfit allows for people to be identified and classified; the unknowable becomes knowable. Here sociologist Pierre Bourdieu's (1984) theory of class reproduction and cultural tastes is useful. He suggests that social structures are complex systems of class cultures comprising sets of lifestyles and cultural tastes, which in turn reproduce class distinction. This can be seen when we look at more contemporary forms of fashion, for not only is class reproduced, so too is race. Bourdieu's theory also illustrates that through class reproduction the status quo is maintained. In other words, social structures are maintained over time through consumption of cultural goods. Blackness is maintained through the consumption of cultural goods associated with essential forms of blackness. Cape Verdean youth adopt the clothing behavior of black America. This can be attributed to the areas in which many Cape Verdeans find themselves living, that is, in close proximity with African Americans. Cape Verdeans then have little opportunity to deviate from the American racialization process and create an identity of their choice. Nonetheless, Cape Verdean youth exhibit tendencies for creating difference within blackness.

WEARING THE FLAG AND CABRAL ON THE BODY

While assembling a black identity through the manifestation of hip-hop fashion, many of my informants also used clothing to communicate and create value in being Cape Verdean. For example, as one informant revealed, while wearing an oversized Partido Africano da Independência de Cabo Verde (PAICV)-imprinted T-shirt and baseball cap, "This [pointing to his shirt] represents who I am: a Cape Verdean in America. . . . It also shows where I'm from. It symbolizes my mentality. . . . It reflects my love for hip-hop." Due to the difficulty of being black in contemporary times, Cape Verdean youth seek ways to construct and maintain a sense of self and dignity.

Although there are various ways in which my informants could exhibit being Cape Verdean, many chose to adorn their bodies with the Cape Verdean flag and/or images of Amílcar Cabral. The wearing of the flag, while a common performative practice at festivals (as noted in the epigraph), was also observed outside the context of Independence Day festivals in the Greater Boston area. Since independence, the national flag of Cape Verde has changed. During the war of liberation and until 1992, the flag of Cape Verde was the same as the revolutionary parties of the Partido Africano da Independência da Guiné e Cabo Verde (PAIGC) and PAICV. The original flag featured a pointed black star, two corn stalks, and a seashell, while green, yellow, and red served as background colors. In 1992, following the electoral victory of the Movimento para Democracia (MpD), a new flag appeared. The colors went from the Pan-African colors of the original to red, blue, and white, and the black star, seashell, and corn stalks were replaced with a circular arrangement of ten gold stars.

In performing blackness, many Cape Verdean youth have turned to the old flag as a statement of personal loyalty to Cape Verde's African heritage, the war of liberation, and the archipelago's spiritual leader Amílcar Cabral, a sign of their Africanity. In discussing the national flags of Cape Verde one informant stated:

As you may know "the powers that be" changed our beloved Cape Verdean flag back in the early 1990s. There are a lot of political reasons for why they did this. One is to align Cape Verde with the European Union. My opinion is that the original flag that Amílcar Cabral designed was more than adequate; it was truth and wisdom towards a united Africa. The African colors in the old flag were significant; African colors reflect our people and our history. Red for the blood, green for the land, gold for the natural resources found in Africa, and black for the people and the essence.

Another anxiously stated:

The change of the color of our flag symbolizes the prostitution of the Cape Verdean government and disrespect for our great hero, Amílcar Cabral. They want to change our African heritage. That flag that looks like the European Union flag is not mine; my flag is what Cabral designed with African colors.

Wearing the old flag on the body expresses an understanding of the relationship between individual and polity, between Africa and the diaspora. The importance of the flag in the imagination of Cape Verdean identity is that it signifies the struggle to choose representations of the polity and assign lasting meaning to them. Wearing the old flag on the body is a central symbol through which a Cape Verdean polity and subjectivity has come to be imagined; it has come to be imagined as an African country, as a nation of black people at odds with a world that does not want them. This could be the result of Cabral's herculean efforts to re-Africanize Cape Verdean people. While some resist wearing the new flag, others have chosen to wear both the old and new flag. As twenty-three-year-old Manny from Brockton stated:

I have tattooed on my back both the old and new flag. The new flag looks, well, new, and the old flag is tattered and torn. I really don't like the new flag, but it's our flag. . . . I prefer the old flag. It represents who we really are and the struggle that we have gone through.

Whether it is the old or new flag, flags on the body are not merely sartorial accessories that go well with sneakers. Rather the Cape Verdean flags as individual bodily symbols tie the wearer to a wider collectivity of people, that is, the Cape Verdean diaspora. In an effort not to dismiss the new flag, despite its lack of popularity among second-generation Cape Verdean youth, a third flag has emerged in the United States, which reflects the growing imagination of Cape Verdean youth identity. This flag, which utilizes the framework of the new flag but the Pan-African colors of the old flag, whether held in the hand or draped over the body is one example of the symbolic (re)construction of Cape Verdean identity. Flags often represent historical unity. However, both the old and new flag, and the emergent third flag, reflect and perpetuate an internal division in the Cape Verdean community. A particular flag membership implies a commitment to a particular reading of Cape Verdean history and identity.

Similarly, T-shirts with the image of Amílcar Cabral on the front have become popular among Cape Verdean youth. Years ago one would be hard pressed to have found Cabral T-shirts. Today, they are ever-present, and Cape Verdean youth are largely responsible. They celebrate a specific racial, ethnic, and political identity in which Cabral is significant.

Amílcar Cabral T-shirts are not so much about the creation of value, but the reproduction of value, the reproduction of his importance to Cape Verdean freedom and self-pride and most importantly as an architect of black revolution. Similar to the image of Argentinean revolutionary Ernesto "Che" Guevara, Cabral shirts communicate the idea of fighting the oppressive and racist system, a system that confronts Cape Verdean youth in the United States. Cabral has become a symbol of romantic and pragmatic rebellion.

Furthermore, the wearing of Cabral T-shirts simultaneously reproduces value in being African and in being black, value in African diasporic relations, relations that Cabral was keen to have observed between colonized African people and oppressed African Americans (see Cabral 1973). Cape Verdean youth wearing Cabral on T-shirts is a confrontation of sorts; it is an interpellative event that calls Cape Verdeans into being. It announces and even enunciates an identity via clothing and stylization. Here it can be argued that Cape Verdean youth have difficulty being interpellated into what Michelle Wright has called a "middle passage epistemology (MPE)" (2010, 72). MPE is the dominant epistemology that structures ways of being black in the United States.

It is an epistemology rooted in the history of the Middle Passage, the crucible of the slave ship. Using Cabral and the war of liberation is one way in which Cape Verdean youth interpellate themselves through another epistemology. They take a different epistemological route, despite having African roots.

Cape Verdean youth also include other, albeit more universally recognizable, black cultural heroes into their sartorial practices, such as Malcolm X and Robert Nesta Marley. Similar to Cabral, both Malcolm X and Bob Marley were political rebels and have become countercultural icons that link black struggles throughout the diaspora, strengthening and fortifying the political ontology of blackness.

Another common sartorial practice of Cape Verdean youth is the use of Pan-African colors in shirts, hats, jewelry, and footwear. Pan-African colors come in two different sets: red, black, and green, and gold, green, and red. The former was popularized by black nationalist Marcus Garvey and later by the nation of Ethiopia. In general, both color sets represent the sociopolitical worldview of Pan-Africanism, an ideology that seeks to unify native Africans with those in diaspora (see Esedebe 1994). The colors are symbolic of global Pan-African blackness. The use of Pan-African colors is especially pronounced among Cape Verdean youth. These colors are dialectically symbolic, for they represent the old flag and the Pan-African colors. The colors bring historical depth and continuity to being black and Cape Verdean, for they are rooted in the black nationalist traditions and the war of liberation.

All efforts at self-representation employ popularized symbols and images of Cape Verdeanness and blackness. Many of the diasporic resources (or symbols) that define blackness are universally recognizable, while those specific to being Cape Verdean are slightly more obscure; however, they do reference symbols of recognition. In other words, the imagery of Amílcar Cabral is not usually left alone, to stand for itself. Rather, it is paired with a symbolic cognate, for instance Malcolm X. Two sets of symbols and symbolic rituals are integrally connected in the construction of Cape Verdean youth identity. At the same time, they serve fundamentally different functions. One set of symbols and symbolic rituals act to demarcate the character and nature of the Cape Verdean community, while simultaneously and strategically distancing it from the African American community. In contrast, the second set of ritual performances are instrumental in the performance of blackness and in developing and sustaining political and strategic links to the African American community more specifically and to global Pan-African blackness more generally.

Put in the context of hip-hop culture this all makes sense. Flags on the body and Cabral shirts do not express a depersonalized sartorial style but the intimate relation, whether real or imagined, to the collectivity. Cape Verdean sartorial style illustrates, as Simmel (1904) suggested over a century ago, the possibility for individual agency, albeit limited by the context of enunciation, and the probabilities of belonging to a wider community and social world. Fashion symbols are indices of one's commitment to the group, its history, its future. The ubiquitous use of these symbols suggests a desire on the part of Cape Verdean youth for greater social cohesion and group affiliation.

CONSTRUCTING A MASCULINE IDENTITY

The fashion styles of both Cape Verdean men and women reflect popular culture in general, but Cape Verdean men seem more attuned to the styles expressed within hip-hop culture. It seems that hip-hop styles resonate more with macho mythologies, and young Cape Verdean men tend to gravitate toward such styles. Hip-hop fashion connotes a racialized masculinity that is the ultimate definition of cool. And as Brian Wilson notes, "black youth are more likely than white youth to define masculine identities through fashion" (1996, 417). Cultural critic Mark Anthony Neal argues, "hip hop has been a primary site for the articulation of distinct forms of black masculinity: urban, hyper-masculine, hyper-sexual, pseudo-criminalized" (2005, 129), a masculinity that capitulates to and instrumentalizes antiblack popular culture.

Amílcar Cabral shirts not only symbolize peace, revolution, and humanity, as described above, but also lend themselves to the construction of a masculine identity. Cabral is seen by Cape Verdean youth as the father of the nation and as a man par excellence. He is the iconic symbol of Cape Verde and Cape Verdean manhood, just as Malcolm X and Huey P. Newton were for many African American men in the 1960s and 1970s.[2] The connection between manhood and revolution was verbally expressed by many Cape Verdean youth. Further, male participants never, formally or informally, acknowledged the role of women in the revolution, nor did the women I interviewed.[3]

The Cape Verdean revolution, like other revolutions before and after the war of liberation, is and continues to be seen as a masculine affair, something undertaken literally and/or metaphorically by men, and what better way to illustrate one's manhood than by wearing a T-shirt imprinted with Cabral's image. Other men of observable prominence in the wardrobe of Cape Verdean men included rappers Tupac Shakur and Biggie Smalls and fictional gangster and hip-hop icons Tony Montana and Alonzo Harris of the movies *Scarface* and *Training Day*. For Cape Verdean youth the importance of such men goes beyond a mere popular culture embrace. Rather it illustrates the embrace of a hypermasculinity that emerges out of heteropatriarchy. For instance, as Greg Dimitriadis suggests, Tupac is seen as "an invincible outlaw who settles his problems swiftly and violently, providing feelings of physical invulnerability to an often intensely vulnerable population" (2001, 102–3). Further, these figures serve as metonyms for the experiences of Cape Verdean youth (Perry 2004). In other words, Tupac, Biggie Smalls, and others bring the male experience to light.

Aside from Cabral T-shirts, other sartorial images that are important are animals, particularly animals of strength and power. More specifically, the image of the lion was often exhibited in the sartorial styles of many Cape Verdean youth. As one participant clearly stated, "The lion represents power and that's why I have lions on my shirts, pants, and sneakers. . . . I got lions on everything." Seconds later he added, "Can you think of anything stronger?" To this end, the lion becomes a metaphor of physical power and control that is often identified with the male body. Young Cape Verdean men, especially those linked to the norms and values of hip-hop culture, seem reluctant to project an image that deviates from this projected masculine norm. Given that animal prowess and masculinity are connected, clothing with animal imprints that fit within the hip-hop fashion system are on the whole easy to find. For example, LRG, Eckō Unltd., and Tuff Gong Clothing all produce garments that feature animals like rhinoceroses and lions.

The utilization of masculine imagery on clothing is an attempt to assemble a legible subjectivity (see hooks 2003; Neal 2013). In the end, young Cape Verdean men fashion their masculine persona through the creative use of symbolic and metonymic accessories. If anything can be gleaned from this, it is that the insistent embrace of authenticity is especially characteristic of struggles to define masculinity.

CAPE VERDEAN ENTREPRENEURIALISM

Fashion has also contributed to creating a culturally mediated economic space. In order for clothing to have value within both the hip-hop community and the Cape Verdean community, wearers must have the appropriate dress and bodily adornments. Thus many entrepreneurs create clothing that conforms to current hip-hop fashion trends. Yet these entrepreneurs are careful to balance their fidelity to Cape Verdean culture with carefully managing its appeal to hip-hop culture writ large. At Cape Verdean cultural festivals, hip-hop gatherings, and entrepreneurial websites, T-shirts, hats, and flags are sold to cater to Cape Verdean youth who desire hip-hop style with Cape Verdean flair. As one clothing entrepreneur of Ten Star Gear proudly and boldly states on his website, "You'll be the freshest banner for Cape Verdean culture!" With a clear hip-hop reference to the importance of place, the site goes on to state, "Let's celebrate our culture. Shout out to all the Cape Verdeans in the states and all over the world!

Wear your style, doesn't matter where you're at, represent where you're from."[4] For many young Cape Verdean entrepreneurs one of the best ways to represent, to show off Cape Verdean pride, is to purchase their apparel. To this end, culture has become a commodity to be bought and sold.

While there is not a wide array of clothing styles available to potential buyers, there are explicit and implied gender-specific styles. As one young entrepreneur stated, "We need to keep our women looking good and the men fresh."[5] The styles of dress for men include short- and long-sleeved T-shirts and fitted baseball caps. Although women could purchase the aforementioned styles, the available sizes, fit, and colors of the shirts and caps are gender-oriented. In keeping with the current hip-hop trend of oversized shirts for men, XXL- and XXXL-sized shirts are common, while small- and medium-sized shirts are absent. Colors include black, army green, blue, white, and gold. Further, much of the clothing reflects a combination of Pan-African colors, red, black, and green. Custom-designed Cape Verdean–specific sneakers offered by Cape Verdean entrepreneurs are also available only in large sizes.

Styles for women are limited. Spaghetti-strapped tank tops, form-fitting T-shirts, and tight short-shorts are the only possibilities. Most of the featured apparel is light in color: light pink, yellow, and white with pink lettering. Tank tops and shorts alike tend to be small and form fitting so as to accentuate the wearer's body type. Noticeably omitted from the styles available for women are the Pan-African colors of red, black, and green. As one participant informed me, "those colors aren't feminine . . . that's why most girls can be seen wearing the new flag . . . those colors [red, white, and blue] are feminine." In this case, femininity, it seems, trumps ethnicity. Also, women's bodies, adorned with the new flag, may signify the creation of a new nation. When asked about the limited options for Cape Verdean women, one Cape Verdean entrepreneur quickly replied, "Women don't wear T-shirts and hats!" There is some truth to this statement, in that any quick glance through a hip-hop culture magazine or visit to any of the number of hip-hop clothing lines that cater to women will show that T-shirts and hats are not part of the current fashion trends for women. Rather, more tailored and complex garments are featured such as bustiers, ruffled blouses, sequin-studded jeans, and halter jumpsuits.

To maximize profits, the clothing styles created not only reflect forms of dress for men and women, but also strongly reference age. The oversized T-shirts, fitted caps, form-fitting shorts, and tank tops speak to youthful desires and a playful exuberance. Thus, while an age-specific and hybridized diasporic identity is constructed, so too are diasporic fashion entrepreneurs. Cape Verdean hip-hop styles are both culturally and economically profitable in the Greater Boston area. While an economic space is created, thus generating income for the creators and sellers, a hybridized diasporic aesthetic is created and maintained. In the end, as sociologist Parminder Bhachu suggests, "the market is not used just as a straightforward mechanism of exchange but also as a means of negotiating a diasporic style, a material form that encodes complex battles of cultural and racial pride" (1999, 48).

POLITICS AND FASHION OF REVOLUTIONARY GLAMOUR

At cultural festivals one becomes aware of the vigilant marketing of the image of Cabral and by extension his political ideas via clothing, which raises this question: Is wearing a Cabral shirt really a political statement? Although a Cabral shirt authenticates a Cape Verdean identity, a political statement in itself, it could be argued that the sociopolitical message of Cabral is muted and silenced, reduced to a specific spectrum of colors and revolutionary imagery and glamor. Similar to other revolutionary figures whose faces have graced cotton T-shirts, some could argue that Cabral has moved from "a politics of liberation to a politics of fashion" (A. Davis 1994, 37). This change in politics, what Cornel West calls a "double bind" (1990, 20), is what confronts all political projects today. However, Todd Boyd sees potential in the double bind. For Boyd, the wearing of revolutionary glamor is where "radical political discourse can critique dominant culture and dominant culture becomes financially viable through the selling of this oppositional discourse" (quoted in Tulloch 2004, 65).

Many of the hip-hop styles adopted by Cape Verdean youth oscillate between protest and mainstream commodity. Cabral T-shirts can keep his memory alive for current and future generations to remember. However, there is also the danger that this memory will become apolitical and ahistorical. In order to resist this temptation, Cape Verdean youth must never substitute the images of Cabral and others for political action, as I outlined in my investigation of Cape Verdean hip-hop music. Cabral's message and iconic status must be incorporated into the current culture of politics and used in new ways so as to ward off political atrophy.

Sadly, and ironically, in order to revive the past and iconic historical figures like Cabral, individuals must turn to the marketplace. Thus, if the market chooses, consciously or unconsciously, to neglect certain aspects of the past, it is left out of the revival and reinvention. The past in this case becomes increasingly fragmented by market forces.

Despite its seemingly growing popularity, I am skeptical that the image of Cabral will become just another floating signifier in the world of commodities. Cabral shirts are probably less likely to die a popular death as we have seen with Che Guevara shirts.

The unlikelihood of this occurrence is due to the small numbers of Cape Verdean youth and the general omission of African revolutionary thinkers from western popular thought. Thus, the countercultural significance of a Cabral shirt may in fact stand the test of time and resist cooption. However, this is not to say that Cape Verdean youth have not and are not capitalizing on the image of Cabral, as I have noted above.

The styles and fashions that many Cape Verdean youth adopt are compensatory and defensive, allowing them to affirm their identities while also affording them some protection in a hostile world. The role of fashion cannot be neglected, for any robust understanding of the construction of race globally must be paired with the practices of everyday life such as fashion and style.

Using the images of Amílcar Cabral, the color sets of Pan-Africanism, and hip-hop fashion trends suggests a performance belonging to a greater community. For example, Cabral and Bob Marley T-shirts cannot simply be seen as T-shirts, but rather as symbols entering into a black dialogue suggesting a shared condition. These images give the clothing worn by Cape Verdean youth a certain significance that possibly does not exist in other sections of society, meaning not duplicated elsewhere. In the end, the sartorial tendencies of second-generation Cape Verdean youth merge content with intent. Sartorial practices serve as badges of identity, expressions of political allegiance and communal values. They are a form of cultural politics, which again tell us something about the culture of antiblack politics. Flags on the body and the image of Cabral are not worn because Cape Verdean youth want to relive the war of liberation or be like Cabral, but because they want the experiences of the war and lessons of Cabral to enhance their own struggle of being black and Cape Verdean in an increasingly troubling and fragmented world.

The Cape Verdean Identity Divide:
A Case of Terminal Blackness

How could you be black on a computer screen?

—Randall Kenan, *Walking on Water*

It's sunny and hot, and hundreds of Cape Verdean youth are in attendance at the Annual Cape Verdean festival in Providence, Rhode Island. I'm excited about meeting several potential participants. However, given the exuberance that develops and the excitement that comes with attending cultural festivals in the middle of the summer when people are spry and high on sunshine, many interested participants had little time to talk. "I'm definitely down," said one potential participant, "but there goes my cousin . . . hit me up on MySpace and we'll connect." Excited, but also disappointed, I continued on only to be told by another would-be participant to check out their MySpace and get back to them. Again, I continued on. I was getting the sense that MySpace and Facebook were much more important than I had originally thought. Later, I was asked if I had a MySpace account, and when I replied "No" the participant responded with an emphatic "you got to get one bro!"[1]

Anxious to start my research, I went home and immediately turned on my computer. I went to MySpace.com and began to browse for people I met at the festival. Informant found! Thus I start with a click of the mouse. The web page begins to load, but before the page loads completely music comes whispering out of my weak desk speakers. The music sounds familiar. I turn up my speakers it is Chachi Carvalho's

"Cape Verdean in America." As the music plays, I bounce my head to the beat of the song while Pan-African colors (i.e., red, black, and green) fill my once black fifteen-inch computer screen. Words and pictures appear next. More specifically, I get a brief biography (and picture) of the creators of the page. I learn where they are from, where they live, their age, marital status, cultural influences, hobbies, and the like. I scroll down, and a montage of photos of black nationalists and revolutionaries such as Amílcar Cabral, Fidel Castro, Malcolm X, and others hang together on the left side of the page. The page is fully loaded, a virtual gallery of sorts, where pictures, biographies, list of friends, and music all clamor for my attention. Tired after a long day in the field (and virtual field), not to mention sensory overload, I sign off, forgetting to create a MySpace account for myself. On the following day I establish a MySpace account.

Self-portraits (or web profiles) such as described above have become digital, crafted from pixels as well as cotton fiber. New communication technologies, cyberspace in particular, have become important mediums for the creation, negotiation, and performance of identity. In this chapter I will discuss how Cape Verdean youth use new communication technologies for identity (re)production. I examine the process by which second-generation Cape Verdean identity was articulated, reified, and renegotiated at MySpace.com, the social networking with a strong music influence. By observing several MySpace pages, I witnessed the process by which members of the Cape Verdean diaspora negotiated the meaning of blackness and Cape Verdeanness, that is, how blackness and Cape Verdeanness are articulated, even embodied, in cyberspace. In other words, I explore the ways in which blackness, identity, technology, and cultural politics are imagined, performed, and assembled in cyberspace. I show how identity is central to the use of new communication technologies like MySpace, not to mention some media sites such as Facebook, YouTube, and Twitter. More specifically, what is being expressed? Is digital media an adjunct to offline subjectivities? To what extend does the Web continue with traditional representational practices? To this end, I juxtapose more traditional spaces for ethnographic observation with a virtual space like MySpace in order to map subtle differences in the construction and performance of identity online. If we are to take identity formation seriously in the twenty-first century, netography will become increasingly more important despite the ephemeral nature of social media.

Cyberscapes and Racial Identity

Over the last three decades, scholarly interest on the relationship between race and technology has grown. The scholastic interest and enthusiasm has reached such a height that the Center for Black Studies at the University of California–Santa Barbara has launched the Race and Technology Project, while also playing host to an international Ford Foundation–sponsored conference (in 2005) entitled "AfroGeeks: Global Blackness and the Digital Public Space." Further, the University of Southern California's Department of American Studies and Ethnicity featured a Summer Institute on Digital Approaches to American Studies and Ethnicity in 2011. Noteworthy texts over the years on the intersections of race and technology include *TechniColor: Race, Technology, and Everyday Life* (Nelson, Tu, and Hines 2001), *Crossing the Digital Divide: Race, Writing, and Technology in the Classroom* (Monroe 2004), *Race, Rhetoric, and Technology: Searching for Higher Ground* (Banks 2005), *Racing Cyberculture: Minoritarian Art and Cultural Politics on the Internet* (McGahan 2008), *Digital Diaspora: A Race for Cyberspace* (Everett 2009), *Race after the Internet* (Nakamura and Chow-White 2012), to name more than a few, and many peer-reviewed journal articles. Initially, most of the work on race and technology and technological practices, known as critical cultural informatics, focuses on the seemingly ever-growing digital divide and potential for remedial initiatives to bring about universal access and participation in new informational technologies for people of color nationally and globally. Another important area of study is in understanding race, representation, and cyberspace.

Issues of access frame many accounts about new communication technologies and race (Graham and Smith 2010). The proverbial digital divide—the troubling gap between those who use computers and the Internet and those who do not—is a ubiquitous trope in most literature concerning race and new technologies (Compaine 2001; Mehra, Merkel, and Bishop 2004, 782; Ragnedda and Muschert 2013). Yet a study by the Pew Internet and American Life Project (2013) suggests that the digital divide is still an issue, but technology trends are changing. The study found that black people are still less likely than white people to go online. However, this does not mean that black people's access to the digital world is limited, for the study also found that black people are more likely than white people to own a mobile phone. Further, the study found that black people are more likely to use social networking sites and update services like Twitter than whites. Internet use has continued to increase regardless of age, class, race, or gender. Further, the population of young online users has grown in recent years and continues to do so. Many of those interviewed participated in a wide range of online activities, from sending e-mails, creating online cultural productions, buying clothing, and Tweeting, to, most importantly, hanging out in social networking sites such as MySpace and Facebook. My informants were frequently online.

If the literature is not talking about the digital divide, it focuses on the leveling effect new technologies may have in creating a society where social constructions such as race, gender, and class matter less. The Internet is viewed as a cyberutopia of sorts, a utopian space where race does not appear; it is where dreams of a postracial world are lived, that is, virtually. People, it seems, are magically freed from the constraints of race. Cyberspace provides the opportunity for people to play with and transcend traditional subjectivities, examples of which are race and gender (see Danet 1998; Florini 2014). As long as one does not reveal his or her body via a visual representation, s/he can play and perform multiple identities online (Nakamura 1999, 2002).[2] For instance, Lisa Nakamura (2002) argues that the Web has allowed surfers to engage in cyber tourism and "play" or perform the role of the other and as result the facticity of the raced body becomes moot. Similarly, Kenneth Thompson argues that "no grand narratives emerge, no one is in control, and there is no ideological closure, it is an ever emerging text" (2002, 411). While the potential to transcend race and to play with racial identity exists in cyberspace, the fact is that race continues to exert its influence as a concept, an idea, a performance in cyberspace (see Nakamura and Chow-White 2012; Everett 2007; Florini 2014; Ignacio 2005; Kolko et al. 2000; McGahan 2008; Nakamura 2002). The performance of race is just as apparent online as it is in person. For instance, there are a plethora of "identity" websites devoted to specific groups and communities (e.g., Blackplanet.com, theRoot.com, blackvoices. com). More importantly, as Jessica Brophy has illustrated in her rejection of cyberutopia, the body, particularly the gendered body, can never and should never be left behind. For her cyberspace is not "a utopian *replacement* for spaces of lived experience, but rather . . . an *augmentation* of those spaces" (Brophy 2010, 932, emphasis original). Instead, it is "bound inseparably into users' lived experiences and embodied agency" (Antebi 2009, 299). With sites like YouTube.com, a video-sharing website where users can upload, share, and watch video clips, visual representations of race and the body are seldom severed. Cyberspace is still a space of black corporeality and embodiment, not noncorporeality and disembodiment. As you will come to see, the *virtual* experience of Cape Verdean youth is strikingly similar to the *real* lived experience.

At the time of this research, MySpace was *the* most popular social networking site in the world. People checked their profiles every day and spent hours updating them. Today, MySpace is a shell of its former self, having been displaced by other social networking sites like Facebook and Twitter and online music sites like Pandora. Nonetheless, what I was able to observe during my field study is instructive, for its popularity may offer insight into identity production that exists on other sites (see S. Sharma 2013).

MySpace is a social networking site that features a profile page and links to friends on the system. Setting up an online identity is fairly simple. Provide your name, address, and e-mail address, after which you are ready to create an online identity. MySpace allows users to personalize their pages by incorporating images, videos, and music that, as I described above, all clamor for the viewer's attention. MySpace users can also blog, that is, provide commentary about current events and/or a particular subject. It also includes a section "About Me" where you can post your name and other physical traits. In short, profiles are personalized to express an individual's tastes, beliefs, and values; it is constructed to give the viewer a sense of who they are.

Once an account is created and constructed, a considerable amount of time is spent updating one's profile—posting comments, blogging, uploading photos and videos, and changing the site's music. However, checking and sending messages constitutes the main activity of users. It is what brings them back every day. This was confirmed by many of my informants: MySpace was part of their everyday lives, which might suggest the division between embodied and virtual subjects is rather tenuous.

MySpace as a part of the everyday life of Cape Verdean youth is methodologically interesting, for my participation in the lives of Cape Verdean youth was limited to cultural festivals, music concerts, and student group performances. Creating a MySpace account allowed me to have a small, albeit virtual, window into the everyday lives of Cape Verdeans. In other words, it was one of few areas where I was able to apply the Geertzian (1973) method of "deep hanging-out."

RACIAL REPRESENTATIONS ONLINE

Performative practices are part of the everyday lives of Cape Verdean youth, be it consuming or producing hip-hop music or dressing the body in a particular way. Through these practices they convey something about their identity, the salient aspects that they want people to see. Cyberspace is another space where Cape Verdean youth use various semiotic resources to convey a racial subjectivity. To this end, my observations suggested that sites like MySpace are far from a refuge from race. Rather, there was little difference between the virtual and the real. Cape Verdean youth created photographic collages of Amílcar Cabral, black nationalists such as Malcolm X and Huey P. Newton, and reggae superstar Bob Marley. They blogged about contemporary political issues salient to black communities such as the "Free Mumia" campaign, the Jena Six case, and the murder of Shawn Bell. And they pasted photos of themselves in the latest hip-hop fashion, often the same clothing I observed them wearing at festivals and other cultural events.

MySpace profiles were just another mechanism by which Cape Verdean youth signaled information about their racial (and ethnic) identity. Thus, cyberspace is not a domain where race ceases to exist, nor is it where "race happens" (Nakamura 2002, xi), for race never just happens. The centrality of race and ethnicity on MySpace could be attributed to several factors. First, MySpace is an image-centered site where photos and videos are prominent features of a user's profile. Posting photos of yourself and others makes one's site attractive to surfers. Therefore, to play with one's racial identity or to become disembodied on MySpace becomes exceedingly difficult given that the body is visually represented. Second, identity on MySpace must be somewhat honest, for it is used not only to meet virtually but also to meet people physically, merging the virtual and the real. MySpace pages are social bulletins of a sort that highlight where one is going, where one is performing, and where one has been. Third, Cape Verdean youth may simply seek continuity between the real and the virtual. This may represent an augmentation of the two where "these technologies become enmeshed in our fleshed bodies" (Brophy 2010, 942). They want to make sure that their racial and ethnic content and intentions are carried out throughout cyberspace. In other words, the process of identity continues in a realm where race, particularly blackness, could be left out. Or could it? Or does the inability to disembody illustrate that the virtual and the real would have to achieve what Judith Butler has called "impossible impermeability" (1999, 170)? This impossibility paired with self-monitoring may highlight what Michel Foucault noted in *Discipline and Punish*, that "he who is subjected to a field of visibility and who knows it, assumes responsibility for the constraints of power; he makes them play spontaneously upon himself; he inscribes in himself the power relation in which he simultaneously plays both roles; he becomes the principle of his own subjection" (1991, 202–3). The dynamics of race as technology are visibly apparent in new communication technologies like MySpace. The virtual identities that I exhibited online gestured increasingly toward blackness as a cultural formation (McGahan 2008). Even though new technologies are an ever-emerging text, a form of consistency remained among Cape Verdean youth, highlighting the social durability of blackness in the twenty-first century.

Cape Verdean Youth and the Virtual Imagined Community

Pace Anita Mannur's insight that "we are in an era of technospheric space, where dislocated geographical points merge and re-pollinate one another in virtual realms," implies cyberspace, then, must be taken seriously when thinking about diasporas (2003, 283). To speak of diaspora or, better yet, to theorize about diaspora without reference to the World Wide Web and other cyberscapes is inadequate and wrongheaded, for many diasporas "are already mediated through cyber and digital scapes" (Mannur 2003, 283). Thus any work on Cape Verdean diasporic identities needs to engage with the Internet. Access to cyberspace allows Cape Verdean youth to connect, albeit in a virtual sense, with others in diaspora and to others in the homeland. Thus the Internet makes diasporic connections to the homeland more intimate than ever before or in ways not possible in the past (see Graziano 2012). The creation of the Internet has allowed for various diasporic zones of alliance to develop (e.g., virtual newspapers). Cape Verdean youth in the Greater Boston area are able to forge communal links in new and exciting ways. With the click of the mouse, touch of the screen, Cape Verdean youth can connect with other Cape Verdeans globally, wherever they are located.

Speaking of her experience and connection with the Papua New Guinean diaspora, Mannur suggests, "the World Wide Web has served as a way to keep those webs of affiliation spinning. We can feel that we were part of a community that is not in danger of becoming an ossified memory" (2003, 285). Similarly, Cape Verdean youth in the Greater Boston area use various social networking sites to connect with other Cape Verdean youth. Further, youth within the archipelago, the geopolitical borders of Cape Verde, are able to connect and reconnect with youth abroad, thus extending their own sense of community. In other words, social networking sites such as MySpace connect users throughout the world, throwing conventional ideas of diaspora into question.

Based on my observations, MySpace helps strengthen a sense of global Pan-African blackness. For instance, it was not uncommon for Cape Verdean youth in the Greater Boston area to have virtual Cape Verdean friends from the archipelago, Portugal, Angola, France, and the Netherlands. As a result, MySpace users may feel the social pressure to be more Cape Verdean when performing their online identities. More importantly, social networking sites promote informal learning, where Cape Verdean youth can learn about Cape Verdean history and historical figures. The MySpace pages that I frequented, for instance, preserved the legacy of Cabral with photos, excerpts from speeches, songs of dedication, and more. Sites often showed amateur footage of trips to the islands, while many sites featured romanticized metaphors of looking back to the past, mainly the war of liberation. These symbols and images create a complex set of metaphors by which Cape Verdean youth live.

MySpace is where social interaction takes place and where common ties are established. New communication technologies serve as an alternative, yet common, source of community in a world comprised of fluid boundaries and displacement. Online discourse helps build cohesion by creating subjectivities rooted in a history and by transmitting culture. A common thread that binds Cape Verdean youth from the Greater Boston area together with other Cape Verdean youth around the world are issues of dispossession and social death. Cape Verdean youth in Amsterdam, Lisbon, Rome, and other places also live in a world filled with antiblackness. MySpace provides a forum where members discuss shared interests and experiences from which they build a sense of belonging to a greater whole and sense of solidarity, which has the potential to manifest itself into collective action (Ebeling 2007). Leonce Gaiter suggests, "The Web could be . . . an extraordinary political tool . . . But only if we are finally willing to forego the dreams of terra firma to which we've hitched our star for all of our postwar history. We must acknowledge that the world into which we so desperately sought entree is dying—and we, like the majority, must embrace new and untested worlds if we are to prosper" (1997). However, Cape Verdean youth have already embraced "new worlds" and have used the Internet to encourage political mobilization and offline social events. In fact, the people who worked for the "Free Tem Blessed" campaign used the Internet to quickly spread information about the arrest and trial of Cape Verdean rapper Tem Blessed.[3] Viewed in this light, new communication technologies are central to a diasporic consciousness and coalition building in the name of blackness. As ships once connected people, now the Internet, microchips and microprocessors, home computers, e-mail, and social networking sites like MySpace connect and re-create a robust sense of self within the matrix of the Cape Verdean diaspora (Gilroy 1995). We must keep in mind, however, that while virtual homelands and diasporic communities may share similarities across oceans and fiber-optic lines, racial identities are specific to location and context, but antiblackness abounds.

In the end, new technologies serve as a means to negotiate and assemble real subjectivities. MySpace identities, more specifically, would cease to exist if not for the plethora of information on and about Cape Verde, images of black revolutionaries, downloadable music, and more. At the hands of its users, pictures of Amílcar Cabral and others can be accessed and pasted as a backdrop for a site's content or used on the periphery of the web page as a revolutionary iconic frame, complete with a social conscious audible from the likes of Tem Blessed and others. If nothing more, new communication technologies such as MySpace and Twitter play a meaningful role in the assemblage of race and other subjectivities, for they provide space for a discourse that articulates the lived experience of black people more generally and Cape Verdean youth more specifically. In other words, the Internet provides a space for Cape Verdean youth to experiment with identity, but not a disembodied identity, where they can share experiences and focus on black history and culture, and ultimately the black condition.

Dark Matters: A Potential (Ante)Politics

I can't say I'm anything but black.... One time I was in Lincoln [a predominantly white suburb of Rhode Island] and kids rolled by me and yell out the window "nigger." ... Even though I'm light skinned.... They're not going to be like he isn't black. He's black! ... That kid called me a "nigger." He didn't care that I was light in tone, that I was Cape Verdean.

—Informant

I have focused on understanding Cape Verdean blackness, exploring how second-generation Cape Verdean youth in the Greater Boston area negotiate and assemble their identity as Cape Verdean and black. In addition, I have explored the tension between conventional and political forms of racial authenticity among Cape Verdean youth. In doing so, I have paid particular attention to the performance of Cape Verdean black subjectivities. This book has been an effort to understand how social agents are racially defined and how they define themselves racially; identity is a socially generated construct, defined by the individual but created with others. *Necessarily Black* is a reflection of the broad and complicated ontologically based experiences of Cape Verdean youth in the Greater Boston area, which by extension hopes to add to an epistemic discourse that converts insight into influence.

My partial accounting of Cape Verdean youth identity has hinged upon three assumptions. First, U.S. ascriptions of blackness rooted in black popular culture, particularly hip-hop culture, inform processes of identity formation among Cape Verdean youth. Second, expressive forms of Cape Verdean youth culture are used as sites where new and old identities of being/becoming/belonging are fashioned and reworked. Third, racialization works to create legible global black identities in order to reinforce global antiblackness. I have tried to offer a more complex and sophisticated mapping than has been hitherto available about Cape Verdean identity. On the one hand, Marilyn Halter (1993) gave us the first sustained work on Cape Verdean identity in the United States. She argued that Cape Verdeans, historically, sit between both registers of race and ethnicity. For her, Cape Verdeans operate and occupy a liminal space, one where racial and ethnic meanings compete. As a result, Cape Verdean identity represents a mix of both racial and ethnic elements. Despite Cape Verdeans being classified as black within the U.S. racial system, Halter emphasizes their ethnic difference over blackness. On the other hand, Sánchez Gibau's (1997, 2005) work argues that Cape Verdeans are actively reshaping race and race relations in the United States by highlighting cultural differences—speaking *kriolu*, eating different foods, listening to different music, and so on. She suggests that normative ideas about race and, by extension, ethnicity are questionable when observing Cape Verdeans in the United States. Both studies privilege the presumed space Cape Verdeans occupy in the black/white binary of the United States. These sentiments are echoed in the following by Naomi Zack:

> An American who identifies herself as mixed black and white race is a new person racially, because old racial categories do not allow her to identify herself this way. It is such a person's very newness racially that gives her the option of racelessness. To be raceless in contemporary racial and racist society is, in effect, to be *anti-race*. If "authenticity" is a definition of the self in the face of oppression, then the authenticity of a person of mixed race may rest on her resistance to biracial categories—the racial authenticity of mixed race could therefore be the racial position of anti-race. (Zack 1993, 164)

This sentiment of being a new person is echoed in the work of Halter, Sánchez Gibau, and others. For these scholars Cape Verdeans occupy the cosmopolitan space popularized by Kwame Anthony Appiah (2007), the liminal space of being raceless. However, such ideas often omit any real discussion about racial identity in relation to social formation and power, that is, the ontological coordinates of society. One gets the sense that both racial (and ethnic) identity at times dissolve, that race and ethnicity as structuring agents reach a vanishing point, which allows individuals to transcend the power of racial classification and by extension racial hierarchies (Bashi 1998).

The problem, or the political folly, with these studies is that while both understand that race persists, they highlight ethnic difference, at the peril of undermining the power of race, particularly antiblackness. For instance, Sánchez Gibau suggests, "Cape Verdeans may enact one 'racialized' identity in the workplace and another 'cultural' identity in the home/enclave environment" (2005, 433). For Sánchez Gibau, a racial identity is employed at the performer's convenience. The insight gained from my informants contradicts such an observation. The lived experience of Cape Verdean blackness is always pronounced, never just conveniently used to accomplish a specific identity. Asserting multiple identities does not necessarily mean challenging and transcending antiblackness and all attendant phenomena. To what extent are challenges made, and how transformative and transcendental are assertions of multiple and mixed identities? How does difference eliminate the power and torque of race? The multiple identities of white people have done little to alter the power and privilege of whiteness (see Ignatiev 1996; Jacobson 1999). The grotesque conditions of inequality in which many Cape Verdean youth find themselves are not the result of cultural difference; rather they are the result of *being* black. Further, the articulation of difference among Cape Verdean youth from the Greater Boston area is the struggle to articulate the black self. My informants have come to think of themselves as black, as suggested in the epigraph, a category that corresponds to an unavoidable social reality that corresponds with social death.

In the adoption of race as a social construction, the import of the body, a material canvas for racial politics, is often lost. In other words, as academics and others have increasingly accepted the social construction of race, the body as a marker of racial importance has lost much of its significance; the materiality of race has fallen to the wayside. Yet my informants consistently remarked that the body, skin color, and hair mark them as black. The aesthetic of blackness is negatively valued. And attached to this difference come cultural connotations and formations. Race is consistently attached to corporeality. As M. A. Doane suggests, "skin becomes the locus of an alienation more acute to the extent that it is inescapable" (1999, 452). Blackness becomes a social fact to the extent that it is a parameter of racial performance being black, in this sense and as illustrated, is parametric (Fanon 1967).

An important conclusion of this study is that in today's world we often speak of race as if it were incorporeal. But of course it is not. Race always shows up attached to the body, clothed or not, virtual or real, in political, spatial, and cultural contexts. It is the context that gives meaning to race. Despite being a social construction, which is always already structured around the paradigmatic, race is physically associated with the body and, as a result, gives meaning to all other performative practices to which it is connected. There is a dialectical relationship between the semiotic (the cultural) and the material (the body). As such, my informants embodied and at times accomplished both thin and thick forms of blackness as a way of being/becoming/belonging. Cape Verdean youth conceive of blackness and its performance in public as centered on experience. Cape Verdean youth in the Greater Boston area move back and forth between the objective, subjective, and intersubjective, but are never without blackness.

Throughout this book, what has been implied is a constant tension between conventional and political forms of racial authenticity. Conventional authenticity is a social device used to project images of truncated forms of blackness. It is steeped in antiblack social life. Examples are black youth as hypermasculine, materialistic, anti-intellectual, and criminal-minded. On the one hand, conventional racial authenticity is the false naturalization of racial identity. It is the performative. As Saidiya Hartman suggests, "the performative has the power to produce the subject that it appears to express" (1997, 57). In this form, blackness is held hostage by antiblackness and white supremacy. On the other hand, the "challenge of blackness" thus requires liberation from essentialized forms of racial identity. Both "cases of blackness" are found in the lived experiences of Cape Verdean youth (Moten 2008).

Despite creative efforts on the part of Cape Verdean youth to highlight difference, to celebrate their Cape Verdeanness, I suggest that racialization is a process that reifies race even as it challenges our thinking about race. More importantly, the outcome illustrates that racialization is a process that ignores difference and forces people into racial categories and hierarchies. For example, as suggested, hip-hop, the blackest of all cultures, plays a crucial role in the meaning-making process. Hip-hop is a site of resistance, a space where difference and engagement are exhibited. Yet it is also a site where narrow subjectivities are cultivated. Many of my informants performed the blackness of the nonblack imagination, blackness in the service of antiblackness and by extension white supremacy.

The assertion of mixed-race identities within an antiblack world means little if *being* black or not still has the power to impact where one lives or dies. What is lost in all of this is that race and ethnicity are intertwined. That is, ethnic identification within the lives of Cape Verdean youth is often racialized, which is to say blackened. Further, blackness as mapped throughout this book exists and is performed through the use of ethnic symbols. These symbols are of a particular kind, that is, they are symbols and signifiers that highlight Cape Verde's African roots, its position within Pan-African blackness.

Race legitimates and gives meaning to social life (and death). Racialization happens in the convergence of the body, physical space, and cultural practices in which Cape Verdean youth engage on a daily basis. While identity is fluid, it does not mean that there are no limitations imposed upon it. One has to feel one belongs to a racial group to feel it is worth investigating in political and cultural events, organizations, and practices on a racial basis. There are structural limitations and self-imposed limitations. While we create society we are also subject to it. For instance, as we have seen, hip-hop culture can sometimes be a means of expressing resistance, but it can also mirror the patterns of dominance from which Cape Verdean youth are seeking refuge. In doing so, truncated forms of blackness are embodied and performed.

From the beginning I set out to map the processes of racialization in order to better understand Cape Verdean blackness. While racialization is often evoked in the negative, it can also be positive. Put differently, embedded in conditions of impossibility is always possibility (Moten 2003, 2008). Racialization in a conceptual sense can be understood as a dialectical process. As anthropologist Leith Mullings has observed, "The modern color line is imposed from above, but also becomes a site for contestation from below" (2004, 1). Given that race is a technological component, a paradigmatic tool of modernity, Cape Verdean youth use blackness in its hegemonic and counterhegemonic forms, calling forth the imperative of both/and. In doing so, they reclaim a little bit of the organizing power of race. Racialization from below uses race also as a tool for organization and political mobilization; it becomes a tool for establishing a sense of belonging.

Racialization from above begets racialization from below, that is, racialization from above creates counterhegemonic social movements. It links the struggle of black people with what is happening in others parts of the world where other dispossessed and racialized people live and *be*. My informants expressed a global Pan-African blackness, and they performed their Cape Verdean identity accordingly. My informants also recognized the fundamental importance of culture and social memory for the mobilization of people. In knowing what it is like to be racialized as black, they turned to Cape Verde neither in search of stagnant cultural practices nor for geographical yearnings of a lost land. Rather, they turned to Cape Verde for political inspiration and solidarity with other oppressed people, but not just any oppressed people, for many of my informants eschewed multiracial solidarity for black solidarity and belonging. To this end, this project was just as much a political project as an intellectual endeavor, in that I set out to understand the complexities and connections of blackness in the twenty-first century. Anyone interested in building successful movements must recognize the fundamental role of antiblackness and not just white supremacy. Now is not the time to state that race no longer matters or subsume and conflate other subjectivities with blackness. Identity politics, and more so a politics of identification, are still relevant because antiblackness is still relevant. Calls for individuals to transcend race are next to impossible when processes of racialization are hard at work. Creating a new world will not be accomplished by appeals to color blindness or the crowding out of black demands. Rather it will be constructed by rethinking race and antiblackness, that is, rethinking the core antagonisms of race in the twenty-first century. People must recognize the multiplicity of experiences and assembled subjectivities, but also be attentive to the context of their enunciations, for the ontic relations create the conditions for the discursive, not the reverse (Hartman 1997).

Race has real effects in determining access to resources; it structures political and social hierarchies and informs the production of knowledge. It shapes the images of self and community. In other words, how one lives their blackness is a choice contingent on specific cultural, political, and socioeconomic circumstances. To this effect, the circumstances of our times do not require an abandonment of race and antiblackness. Instead they require the unrelenting critique of antiblackness as constitutive of modernity, of the supposed "postracial" and "postblack" temporality in which we live. Identity is contingent, fluid, diachronic, and so on, but the specter of race lurks in the background. Racial identity in its essentialized and fluid forms are aspects of the lived realities of Cape Verdean youth in the Greater Boston area. *Necessarily Black* is more about the structuring logic of antiblackness that defines the scope and quality of *being* in the world. It shows how second-generation Cape Verdean youth in the Greater Boston area, racialized as black people, are affected by race and actively structure their existence around its reality. In short, we must continue to investigate the significance of racialization in the lives of those defined as "black," while always being attentive to the structuring logic of antiblackness.

My informants' understanding of what it means to be black in the United States is informed by their relationships with peers and their marginalized positions in larger society. They embrace a black subjectivity. Second-generation Cape Verdean youth inhabit blackness suspended in the public imaginary and popular cultural portrayals of blacks. African descent still holds a great deal of weight as totalizing criteria for social categorization. While they assert a black identity, they also express a strong sense of ethnic solidarity. Like other dispossessed people, they are re-creating identities under unequal relations of power. Cape Verdean youth recognize that they are seen as racialized "others," as blackened subjects, and they have responded to racial exclusion and inequality by adopting and embracing their blackness. The racialization of Cape Verdean youth must be understood as an ongoing process of the articulation of blackness both in its homogenized nonhistoricized form and its multiple fluid forms. Many Cape Verdean youth illustrated the dialectical tension between a self caught in its production by racial structures yet holding the potential to recognize and act against this production. In other words, Cape Verdean youth illustrate the tension between the indicative and subjective. Despite showing levels of agency, racial structures have a structuring effect on identity, that is, they call you into being. First-generation Cape Verdeans often highlighted the inadequacies of modernist racial categories and the binary approach to race. However, those concerns do not necessarily remain among Cape Verdean youth. I say *necessarily* because those Cape Verdean youth interviewed often wished not to be restricted to the black/nonblack binary. Yet they understood the social force of antiblackness. In other words, while some participants sought to move beyond binary racial categories in their self-identificatory practices, this did not lead to an erasure of blackness in their thinking and being.

Echoing W. E. B. Du Bois, Cape Verdeans are both contingently and necessarily black. Cape Verdean youth recognize that to be just Cape Verdean is a form of self-deception. To do otherwise is to elide the racial and gesture toward racial nihilism. Cape Verdean youth see the body and its social markings. Many Cape Verdean youth are aware of being "mixed." In fact, claiming to be Cape Verdean is a declaration/expression of being mixed, of being different, yet of being black. In the end, what we get with Cape Verdean youth is a deeper understanding that blackness is simultaneously local and particular as well as global and universal. As Aimé Césaire (2000) points out, all black subjects are constantly moving between subject and object. To borrow Anna Tsing's (2005) metaphor "friction," the friction that is the result of living in the world gives way to new ways of being black, which by extension helps recalibrate political struggles, that is, to become aware of previously unrecognized connections and realities. Black solidarity, materially speaking, may help expand participation in various political arenas.

Processes of racialization have expanded and continue to police and discipline culturally/politically distinctive forms of self-definition. In the end, racial identity as illustrated by Cape Verdean youth highlights the constitutive antagonism (Žižek 2005) of racial identity. While this may not sit well with many, the reality is that we cannot reconcile the antagonism; we can only "suture" it. This, in the end, is the *real* of racial identity. Nonetheless, mapping racial subjectivities in the twenty-first century is important. Our work on race, racial identity, racial hierarchies, antiblackness, and processes of racialization are far from over and complete. Thus I urge that we continue to produce dynamic and illuminating accounts of antiblackness, so that we can move forward and create a new world, but one not of this world. Given this reality it might be wise to end with Cabral's powerful words: "Hide nothing from the masses of our people. Tell no lies. Expose lies whenever they are told. Mask no difficulties, mistakes, failures. Claim no easy victories" (1973, 72). In other words, freedom here and now must be absolute not relative. Whether or not *Necessarily Black* speaks to the lived experience of Cape Verdean youth as a whole is less important than the view it opens onto race and blackness and the questions it enables us to ask about the durability and reach of antiblackness.

Notes

PREFACE

1. Freestyle rap is an improvisational form of rapping, performed with little or no previously composed lyrics.

2. Cape Verdean creole is also known as *kriolu*, *crioulo*, and *kabuverdianu*.

3. Here I am referring to the "structure of feeling" in the way in which Raymond Williams makes plain in *Marxism and Literature* (1977), that is, to take what we do as conscious and deliberately acting individuals as a model for how we conduct ourselves in everyday life.

INTRODUCTION

1. Books that map this phenomenon include, but are not limited to, Arthur (2000, 2010), Greer (2013), Okpewho and Nzegwu (2009), and Stoller (2002).

2. Interestingly, as Jemima Pierre observes in her brilliantly composed book *The Predicament of Blackness: Postcolonial Ghana and the Politics of Race*, "discussions of the 'Black experience' often . . . [do] not include contemporary Black *African* experience, even as it is clear that continental Africans have always been and continue to be racialized as 'Black' in a global racial order that denigrates Blackness and exploits and dehumanizes Black people" (2013, xiv).

3. Racial studies often implicitly and explicitly attempt to deontologize race. Paul Gilroy (2001) is just one of many scholars that try to unhinge race from its ontological foundation.

4. See for example Batiste 2012; Bolden 2008; Clay 2003; Dimitriadis 2001; Fleetwood 2010;

Forman 2001; Ongiri 2009.

5. *Necessarily Black* is inspired by one of the few ethnographies to deal with antiblackness: Vargas 2006.

6. Much of the contemporary work on racial identity focuses on an ensemble of questions: How does diaspora and transnationalism complicate understandings of racial identity? How does one (or a community) negotiate dualities and multiplicities when belonging to more than one race or culture? What are the implications of identities that transgress racial and/or national lines? As Frank Wilderson notes, "the academy's ensembles of questions are fixated on specific and 'unique' experiences of the myriad identities. . . . This would be fine if the work led us back to a critique of the paradigm; but most of it does not" (2010, 6).

7. For a clear and analytically rigorous investigation into the social construction of race, see Haslanger 2012.

8. According to philosopher Lewis Gordon, blackness is a "hole in being" (1995a, 124), a "form of nothing" (105), and a "black whole" (99).

9. Racial formation is understood as changes to forms of racial identity and subjectivity over time; race comes into being as the effect of interconnected social actions. This results in racial formation having particular ontological characteristics, which goes undefined by Omi and Winant. First, racial formation has a certain durability and stability, at times the result of the continued performance and embodiment of race. Second, racial formation is always rooted in a concrete spatiotemporal location. In other words, all racial formations have an undergirding paradigm, and in this case, as supported by my participants' insights, it is antiblackness. To this Jared Sexton adds, "the foreclosure of blackness from the prospects and preoccupations of the modern world, the constitutive exclusion of blacks from the realm of 'humanity,' hierarchies and all, can certainly be thought in ontological terms. Perhaps its structural manifestations should at least be considered *quasi-ontological*. This nomination would have to do with both the breathtaking historical longevity of antiblackness—whether one dates its emergence proper in the eighteenth century, the sixteenth century, or the thirteenth century—and its basic coextension with the culture and politics of modernity" (2008, 244–45).

CHAPTER 1. MAKING SENSE OF LIGHT-SKIN AFRICAN BLOOD:
THE GRAMMAR OF CAPE VERDEAN IDENTITY

1. Ronald R. Sundstrom argues that "Mixed race identity is based on mixed race experience. . . . Mixed race identity results from the positioning of individuals in social spaces where they experience, as members of multiple racial groups, various combinations of the social forces that make race and the various racial groups real. The racial or experiential purity of parent groups, of blackness, whiteness, and so on does not follow from the claim that mixed race identity is possible" (2001, 299–300).

2. Recently, Cape Verdean identity has featured as a topic at the biannual Critical Mixed Race Studies Conference at DePaul University.

3. For an extended treatment on Cape Verdean history see Lobban and Saucier 2007. See also Lobban 1995.

4. The interconnectivity and interdependence between nation-state and diaspora is so impor-

tant that the government of Cape Verde established a department that is attentive to issues affecting the diaspora and its emigrants. The effectiveness of such a program remains to be seen.

5. "Cape Verdean" as an option was added to the 1980 census and was subsequently dropped.

6. This complex system of racial classification is similar to the ways Brazilians are racially classified; see Telles 2004.

7. Self-identifying as "Portuguese" rather than Cape Verdean has persisted, although constantly challenged by younger Cape Verdeans. Such designation is a remnant of colonialism.

8. Seminal works in mixed race studies include Anzaldúa 1987; Root 1992 and 1996; and Zack 1995. For critical mixed race studies, see Gordon 1995b.

9. Liminality is central to many postcolonial critiques, that is, central to postcolonial becoming.

10. My use of Perea (1997) and Alcoff (2006, 2013) is simply symptomatic of this scrutiny.

11. For an in-depth analysis on the circulation and robustness of antiblackness within Asian American communities in the United States, see Nopper 2011.

CHAPTER 2. BODY AND BEING: NOTES ON CAPE VERDEAN BLACKNESS IN AMERICA

1. See the visually stunning Blay and Theard 2013.

2. See also Ibrahim 2014.

3. See also Neal 2001 and George 2005.

4. Philosopher Charles Mills proffers a similar idea of blackness in *The Racial Contract* (1998).

5. Although far too numerous to list, some fitting examples of what Kelley calls ghetto ethnography include Rainwater 1970, Hannerz 1969, and Schulz 1969.

6. Ethnicity in its most fundamental form is a concept referring to a shared way of life as reflected in specific cultural practices. It is, as David Theo Goldberg suggests, "the mode of cultural identification and distinction" (1993, 74). African American ethnicity, for instance, draws "on the syncretic cultural heritage created by diverse African ethnic groups and do[es] so within the distinctly American religious milieu of an overarching American civil religion" (Hill Collins 2006, 79). Comparatively speaking, race is defined on the basis of "the rhetoric of descent," while ethnicity is socially defined on the basis of "the rhetoric of cultural consent" (Goldberg 1993, 75–76). Racial designation often refers to appearance and aptitude; ethnicity has none of these connotations. According to Stephen Cornell and Douglass Hartmann (1998), ethnicity is internally asserted, whereas race is externally imposed. It is reasonable to assume then, that race is also a power relation, whereas ethnicity is not. In other words, ethnicity, for Cornell and Hartmann, is not necessarily exploitative, hierarchical, and conflictual, as is race. Ethnicity is nonhierarchical, but only as far as it is unrelated to race. Ethnicity is more about inclusion than exclusion. However, the constitutive elements that comprise a particular ethnic group change over time.

7. All informants' names have been changed to protect their anonymity.

8. Here I am reminded of when Fanon limns, "In the beginning I wanted to confine myself to the Antilles." He continues, "regardless of consequences, dialectic took the upper hand and I was compelled to *see* that the Antillean is first of all a Negro" (Fanon 1967, 172–73, emphasis

original).

9. "Providence Neighborhood Profiles."

10. "Being country" as opposed to "being urban" is at the vortex of southern definitions of black-ness. Any number of popular hip-hop songs from the south in the past decade is illustrative of this point.

CHAPTER 3. *KRIOLU* NOIZE: BRIDGES OF BLACK CAPE VERDEAN SOUND

1. To this Robin Means Coleman adds "If you *don't* enter into hip hop culture, then you are open to Huxtable-esque criticisms of facilitating modern racism" (2006, 86).

2. D. Lopes, "Track 4," *Concrete Intelligence Sample*, Street Smart Entertainment, 2007.

3. Chachi has since performed in Cape Verde as well as shot multiple music videos in the islands.

4. The Game, *The Documentary*, Aftermath/G-Unit/Interscope Records, 2004. The beginning of the second verse, which Tem Blessed signifies on, is as follows: "I had dreams of fuckin an R&B bitch like Maya / When I saw dat ass on the front of that King / Read the article in a magazine / She loved gangsters, loved nasty things / So I'm the glass house havin' nasty dreams."

5. David Banner, *Certified*, Universal Records, 2005.

6. For Peter McLaren, "rap [also] helps to communicate symbols and meanings and articulates intersubjectively the lived experience of social actors. The ontological status of the . . . rapper resides in the function of the commodity of blackness, but a certain quality of blackness that is identified through expressive codes of the rapper is the 'inner turmoil' of the oppressed black subject of history" (1997, 171).

7. From 3rd Eye Unlimited website, www.3rdeyeunlimited.com/.

CHAPTER 4. CAPE VERDEAN YOUTH COOL: TAILORING IDENTITY

1. I am not suggesting that all working-class and poor people shop at Walmart, nor am I say-ing all wealthy people wear Armani suits and Salvatore Ferragamo shoes. However, the price discrepancy between shoes from Walmart, for instance, and shoes by Ferragamo suggests that only wealthy people can afford the latter.

2. Both Malcolm X and Huey P. Newton still hold sway over black youth, but their symbolic sig-nificance was no doubt at its apogee in the 1960s and 1970s.

3. This omission should be seen as a result of historical neglect. Historians have, in fact, noted the role of women in the revolution. See Urdang 1979.

4. The website for Ten Star Gear no longer exists. However, it was formerly located at http://tenstarcv.com/TenStar_Gear.html.

5. Here I read "our" as referring to Cape Verdean women, not as a personal possession.

CHAPTER 5. THE CAPE VERDEAN IDENTITY DIVIDE: A CASE OF TERMINAL BLACKNESS

1. Initially, I thought social networking sites like MySpace, Friendster, Bebo, Facebook, and others were nothing more than technologically advanced versions of Internet chat rooms, where spammers, computer nerds, and teenagers virtually hung out.

2. Lisa Nakamura provides us with the term "identity tourism," which describes the process where one plays with an identity that would not be ascribed offline. As she states, "[in] cyberspace players do not ever need to look for jobs or housing, compete for classroom attention, or ask for raises. This ensures that identity tourists need never encounter situations in which exotic otherness could be a liability, an aspect of racial passing on the Internet that contributes to its superficiality" (Nakamura 2002, 56).

3. Tem Blessed was arrested, abused, and detained by Massachusetts State Police. He was charged with resisting arrest, threatening to commit a crime, malicious destruction of property over $250, disorderly conduct, and assault and battery on a police officer. A campaign was started accusing the police of racial profiling and police brutality.

References

Abdullah, Zain. 2009. "African 'Soul Brothers' in the 'Hood: Immigration, Islam, and the Black Encounter." *Anthropological Quarterly* 82, no. 1: 37–62.

Alcoff, Linda Martin. 2006. *Visible Identities: Race, Gender, and the Self*. New York: Oxford University Press.

——. 2013. "Afterword: The Black/White Binary and Antiblack Racism." *Critical Philosophy of Race* 1, no. 1: 121–24.

Allman, Jean, ed. 2004. *Fashioning Africa: Power and the Politics of Dress*. Bloomington: Indiana University Press.

Anderson, Elijah. 1992. *Streetwise: Race, Class, and Change in an Urban Community*. Chicago: University of Chicago Press.

Antebi, Susan. 2009. "The Talk Show Uploaded: YouTube and the Technicity of the Body." *Social Identities* 15, no. 3: 297–311.

Anzaldúa, Gloria. 1987. *Borderlands/La Frontera: The New Mestiza*. San Francisco: Aunt Lute Books.

Appiah, Kwame Anthony. 2007. *Cosmopolitanism: Ethics in a World of Strangers*. New York: W. W. Norton.

Appiah, Kwame Anthony, and Amy Gutmann. 1996. *Color Conscious: The Political Morality of Race*. Princeton: Princeton University Press.

Aranke, Sampada. 2013. "Fred Hampton's Murder and the Coming Revolution." *Trans-Scripts* 3: 116–38.

Arthur, John A. 2000. *Invisible Sojourners: African Immigrant Diaspora in the United States*. Westport, CT: Praeger.

——. 2010. *African Diaspora Identities: Negotiating Culture in Transnational Migration*. Lanham, MD: Lexington Books.

Asante, M. K., Jr. 2009. *It's Bigger than Hip-Hop: The Rise of the Post-Hip-Hop Generation*. New York: St. Martin's Griffin.

Asante, Molefi Kete. 2005. *Race, Rhetoric, and Identity: The Architecton of Soul*. Amherst, NY: Humanity Press.

Banks, Adam. 2005. *Race, Rhetoric, and Technology: Searching for Higher Ground*. New York: Routledge.

Barnard, Malcolm. 2002. *Fashion as Communication*. New York: Routledge.

Barrett, Lindon. 1998. *Blackness and Value: Seeing Double*. Cambridge: Cambridge University Press.

———. 2014. *Racial Blackness and the Discontinuity of Western Modernity*. Urbana: University of Illinois Press.

Barthes, Roland. 1967. *The Fashion System*. New York: Hill.

Bashi, Vilna. 1998. "Racial Categories Matter because Racial Hierarchies Matter: A Commentary." *Ethnic and Racial Studies* 21, no. 5: 959–68.

Batalha, Luís. 2004. *The Cape Verdean Diaspora in Portugal: Colonial Subjects in a Postcolonial World*. Lanham, MD: Lexington Books.

Batalha, Luís, and Jørgen Carling, eds. 2008. *Transnational Archipelago: Perspectives on Cape Verdean Migration and Diaspora*. Amsterdam: Amsterdam University Press.

Batiste, Stephanie Leigh. 2012. *Darkening Mirrors: Imperial Representation in Depression-Era African American Performance*. Durham: Duke University Press.

Beleza, Sandra, Joana Campos, Jailson Lopes, Isabel Inês Araújo, Ana Hoppfer Almada, António Correia e Silva, Esteba J. Parra, and Jorge Rocha. 2012. "The Admixture Structure and Genetic Variation of the Archipelago of Cape Verde and Its Implications for Admixture Mapping Studies." *PLOS/One*. November 30.

Beleza, Sandra, Nicholas A. Johnson, Sophie I. Candille, Devin M. Absher, Marc A. Coram, Jailson Lopes, Joana Campos, Isabel Inês Araújo, Tovi M. Anderson, Bjarni J. Vilhjálmsson, Magnus Nordborg, António Correia e Silva, Mark D. Shriver, Jorge Rocha, Gregory S. Barsh, and Hua Tang. 2013. "Genetic Architecture of Skin and Eye Color in an African-European Admixed Population." *PLOS/Genetics*. March 21.

Bennett, Lerone. 1972. *The Challenge of Blackness*. Chicago: Johnson Publishing.

Bhabha, Homi. 1986. "Foreword: Remembering Fanon." In Frantz Fanon, *Black Skin, White Masks*, vii–xxvi. London: Pluto Press.

Bhachu, Parminder. 1999. "Diaspora Politics through Style: Racialized and Politicized Fashion in Global Markets." In *Performativity and Belonging*, ed. Vikki Bell, 42–59. London: Sage.

Biko, Steve. 2002. *I Write What I Like: Selected Writings*. Chicago: University of Chicago Press.

Blay, Yaba, and Noelle Theard. 2013. *(1)ne-Drop: Shifting the Lens on Race*. Philadelphia: Black Print Press.

Bogues, Anthony. 2012. "And What About the Human? Freedom, Human Emancipation, and the Radical Imagination." *boundary 2* 39, no. 3 (fall): 29–46.

Bolden, Tony. 2008. *The Funk Era and Beyond: New Perspectives on Black Popular Culture*. New York: Palgrave Macmillan.

Bourdieu, Pierre. 1984. *Distinction: A Social Critique of the Judgment of Taste*. Cambridge, MA: Harvard University Press.

Brophy, Jessica E. 2010. "Developing a Corporeal Cyberfeminism: Beyond Cyberutopia." *New Media*

& Society 12, no. 6: 929–45.

Brubaker, Rogers, and Fredrick Cooper. 2000. "Beyond 'Identity.'" *Theory and Society* 29: 1–47.

Burtenshaw, Rónán. *2012*. "Raceocracy: An Interview with Barnor Hesse—Part 1." *Irish Left Review*, October 24.

Butler, Judith. 1999. *Gender Trouble: Feminism and the Subversion of Identity*. New York: Routledge.

Cabral, Amílcar. 1973. *Return to the Source: Selected Speeches of Amilcar Cabral*. New York: Monthly Review Press.

Cacho, Lisa Marie. 2012. *Social Death: Racialized Rightlessness and the Criminalization of the Unprotected*. New York: New York University Press.

Calefato, Patrizia. 2004. *The Clothed Body*. Oxford: Berg Publishers.

Carling, Jørgen. 2002. "Migration in the Age of Involuntary Immobility: Theoretical Reflections and Cape Verdean Experiences." *Journal of Ethnic and Migration Studies* 28, no. 1: 5–42.

Carter, Greg. 2013. *The United States of the United Races: A Utopian History of Racial Mixing*. New York: New York University Press.

Certeau, Michel de. 1984. *The Practice of Everyday Life*. Berkeley: University of California Press.

Césaire, Aimé. 2000. *Discourse on Colonialism*. New York: Monthly Review Press.

Challinor, Elizabeth. 2013. "Home and Overseas: The Janus Faces of Cape Verdean Identity." *Diaspora* 17, no. 1: 84–104.

Chandler, Robin M., and Nuri Chandler-Smith. 2005. "Flava in Ya Gear: Transgressive Politics and the Influence of Hip-Hop on Contemporary Fashion." In *Twentieth-Century American Fashion*, ed. Linda Welters and Patricia A. Cunningham, 229–54. Oxford: Berg Publishers.

Clark, Msia Kibona. 2008. "Identity among First and Second Generation African Immigrants in the United States." *African Identities* 6, no. 2 (May): 169–81.

Clay, Andreana. 2003. "Keepin' It Real: Black Youth, Hip Hop Culture, and Black Identity." *American Behavioral Scientist* 46, no. 10 (June): 1346–58.

——. 2012. *The Hip-Hop Generation Fights Back: Youth, Activism, and Post-Civil Rights Politics*. New York: New York University Press.

Coli, Waltraud Berger, and Richard A. Lobban. 1990. *The Cape Verdeans in Rhode Island: A Brief History*. Providence: Rhode Island Publications Society.

Compaine, Benjamin M. 2001. *The Digital Divide: Facing a Crisis or Creating a Myth?* Cambridge, MA: MIT Press.

Cooper, Carolyn. 2004. *Sound Clash: Jamaican Dancehall Culture at Large*. New York: Palgrave-Macmillan.

Copeland, Huey. 2013. *Bound to Appear: Art, Slavery, and the Site of Blackness in Multicultural America*. Chicago: University of Chicago Press.

Cornell, Stephen, and Douglas Hartmann. 1998. *Ethnicity and Race: Making Identities in a Changing World*. Thousand Oaks, CA: Pine Forge Press.

Damhorst, Mary Lynn, Kimberly A. Miller-Spillman, and Susan O. Michelman. 2005. *The Meanings of Dress*. New York: Fairchild Publications.

Danet, Brenda. 1998. "Text as Mask: Gender, Play, and Performance on the Internet." In *CyberSociety 2.0: Revisiting Computer-Mediated Communication and Community*, ed. Steven G. Jones, 129–58. Thousand Oaks, CA: Sage.

Da Silva, Denise Ferreira. 1998. "Facts of Blackness: Brazil Is Not Quite the United States . . . and Racial Politics in Brazil?" *Social Identities* 4, no. 2: 201–34.

———. 2007. *Toward a Global Idea of Race*. Minneapolis: University of Minnesota Press.

Davidson, Basil. 1990. *The Fortunate Isles: A Study in African Transformation*. Trenton: Africa World Press.

Davis, Angela Y. 1994. "Afro Images: Politics, Fashion, and Nostalgia." *Critical Inquiry* 21, no. 1: 37–45.

Davis, Mike. 2006. *Planet of Slums*. New York: Verso.

Delgado, Richard. 1998. "The Black/White Binary: How Does It Work?" In *The Latino/a Condition: A Critical Reader*, ed. Richard Delgado and Jean Stefancic, 369–75. New York: New York University Press.

Deliovsky, Katerina, and Tamari Kitossa. 2013. "Beyond Black and White: When Going Beyond May Take Us Out of Bounds." *Journal of Black Studies* 44, no. 2: 158–81.

Denton, Nancy. 1994. "Residential Segregation: Challenge to White America." *Journal of Intergroup Relations* 21, no. 2 (summer): 19–35.

Dimitriadis, Greg. 2001. *Performing Identity/Performing Culture: Hip Hop as Text, Pedagogy, and Lived Practice*. New York: Peter Lang.

Doane, Mary Ann. 1999. "Dark Continents: Epistemologies of Racial and Sexual Difference in Psychoanalysis and the Cinema." In *Visual Culture: The Reader*, ed. Jessica Evans and Stuart Hall, 448–56. London: Sage.

Drake, St. Clair, and Horace R. Cayton. 1962. *Black Metropolis: A Study of Negro Life in a Northern City*. New York: Harper and Row.

Duarte, Dulce Amada. 1984. "The Cultural Dimension in the Strategy for National Liberation: The Cultural Bases of the Unification Between Cape Verde and Guinea-Bissau." *Latin American Perspectives* 11, no. 2 (Spring): 55–66.

Du Bois, W. E. B. 1897. *The Conservation of Races*. American Negro Academy Occasional Papers 2. Washington, DC: American Negro Academy.

———. 1899[1996]. *The Philadelphia Negro: A Social Study*. Philadelphia: University of Pennsylvania Press.

Ebeling, M. 2007. "The New Domain: Black Agency in Cyberspace." *Radical History Review* 87: 96–108.

Eglash, Ron. 1999. *African Fractals: Modern Computing and Indigenous Design*. New Brunswick, NJ: Rutgers University Press.

Ehlers, Nadine. 2012. *Racial Imperatives: Discipline, Performativity, and Struggles Against Subjection*. Bloomington: Indiana University Press..

Elam, Harry J., Jr., and Kennell Jackson, eds. 2005. *Black Cultural Traffic: Crossroads in Global Performance and Popular Culture*. Ann Arbor: University of Michigan Press.

Esedebe, P. Olisanwuche. 1994. *Pan-Africanism: The Idea and Movement, 1776–1991*, 2nd ed. Washington DC: Howard University Press.

Everett, Anna, ed. 2007. *Learning Race and Ethnicity: Youth and Digital Media*. Cambridge, MA: MIT Press.

———. 2009. *Digital Diaspora: A Race for Cyberspace*. Albany: SUNY Press.

Eversley, Shelly. 2004. *The Real Negro: The Question of Authenticity in Twentieth-Century African American Literature*. New York: Routledge.

Fanon, Frantz. 1963. *The Wretched of the Earth*. New York: Grove Press.

———. 1967. *Black Skin, White Masks*. New York: Grove Press.

Farley, Anthony. 1997. "The Black Body as Fetish Object." *Oregon Law Review* 76, no. 3: 457–535.

Fernandes, Sujatha. 2011. *Close to the Edge: In Search of the Global Hip Hop Generation*. New York: Verso.

Fikes, Kesha. 2009. *Managing African Portugal: The Citizen-Migrant Distinction*. Durham, NC: Duke University Press.

Fleetwood, Nicole R. 2010. *Troubling Vision: Performance, Visuality, and Blackness*. Chicago: The University of Chicago Press.

Florini, Sarah. 2014. "Tweets, Tweeps, and Signifyin': Communication and Cultural Performance on 'Black Twitter.'" *Television and New Media* 5, no. 3: 223–37.

Foner, Nancy, ed. 2013. *One Out of Three: Immigrant New York in the Twenty-First Century*. New York: Columbia University Press.

Forman, Murray. 2001. "'Straight Outta Mogadishu': Prescribed Identities and Performative Practices among Somali Youth in North American High Schools." *Topia* 5: 33–60.

———. 2002. *The 'Hood Comes First: Race, Space, and Place in Rap and Hip-Hop*. Middletown, CT: Wesleyan University Press.

Foucault, Michel. 1991. *Discipline and Punish: The Birth of the Prison*. Harmondsworth: Penguin.

Foy, Colm. 1988. *Cape Verde: Politics, Economy, and Society*. New York: Pinter Publishers.

Freyre, Gilberto. 1953. *Aventura e rotina: sugestões de uma viagem à procura das constantes portuguesas de caráter e ação*. Rio de Janeiro: Jose Olympio.

Gaiter, Leonce. 1997. "Is the Web Too Cool for Black People?" *Salon Magazine*, June 5.

Garfinkel, Harold. 1967. *Studies in Ethnomethodology*. Englewood Cliffs, NJ: Prentice Hall.

Geertz, Clifford. 1973. *The Interpretation of Cultures: Selected Essays*. New York: Basic Books.

George, Nelson. 2005. *Post-Soul Nation: The Explosive, Contradictory, Triumphant, and Tragic 1980s as Experienced by African Americans (Previously Known as Blacks and before that Negroes)*. New York: Viking-Penguin.

Gilroy, Paul. 1995. *The Black Atlantic: Modernity and Double Consciousness*. Cambridge, MA: Harvard University Press.

———. 2001. *Against Race: Imagining Political Culture Beyond the Color Line*. Cambridge, MA: Harvard University Press.

Góis, Pedro. 2010. "Cape Verdeanness as a Complex Social Construct: Analysis of Ethnicity through Complexity Theory." In *Identity Processes and Dynamics in Multi-Ethnic Europe*, ed. Charles Westin, José Bastos, Janine Dahinden, and Pedro Góis, 257–78. Amsterdam: Amsterdam University Press.

Goldberg, David Theo. 1993. *Racist Culture: Philosophy and the Politics of Meaning*. Malden, MA: Blackwell.

———. 1997. *Racial Subjects: Writing on Race in America*. New York: Routledge.

———. 2002. *The Racial State*. Malden, MA: Blackwell.

Gonçalves, R., A. T. Fernandes, and A. Brehm. 2004. "Cabo Verde Islands: Different Maternal and Paternal Heritage Testifies the Nature of Its First Settlers." *International Congress Series* 1261:372–73.

Gordon, Lewis R. 1995a. *Bad Faith and Antiblack Racism*. Atlantic Highlands, NJ: Humanities Press.

——. 1995b. "Critical 'Mixed Race'?" *Social Identities* 1, no. 2: 381–95.

——. 1997. *Her Majesty's Other Children: Sketches of Racism from a Neocolonial Age*. Lanham, MD: Rowman & Littlefield.

——. 2000. *Existentia Africana: Understanding Africana Existential Thought*. New York: Routledge.

——. 2007. *Disciplinary Decadence: Living Thought in Trying Times*. Boulder: Paradigm Press.

Gott, Suzanne, and Kristyne Loughran, eds. 2010. *Contemporary African Fashion*. Bloomington: Indiana University Press.

Graham, Roderick, and Danielle T. Smith. 2010. "Dividing Lines: An Empirical Examination of Technology Use and Internet Activity among African Americans." *Information, Communication, and Society* 13, no. 6: 892–908.

Gray, Herman. 2004. *Watching Race: Television and the Struggle for Blackness*. Minneapolis: University of Minnesota Press.

——. 2005. *Cultural Moves: African Americans and the Politics of Representation*. Berkeley: University of California Press.

Graziano, Teresa. 2012. "The Tunisian Diaspora: Between 'Digital Riots' and Web Activism." *Social Science Information* 54, no. 4: 534–50.

Greer, Christina M. 2013. *Black Ethnics: Race, Immigration, and the Pursuit of the American Dream*. New York: Oxford University Press.

Halter, Marilyn. 1993. *Between Race and Ethnicity: Cape Verdean American Immigrants, 1860–1965*. Urbana: University of Illinois Press.

Hannerz, Ulf. 1969. *Soulside: Inquires into Ghetto Culture and Community*. New York: Columbia University Press.

——. 1987. "The World in Creolization." *Africa* 57, no. 4: 546–59.

Harney, Stefano, and Fred Moten. 2013. *The Undercommons: Fugitive Planning & Black Study*. London: Minor Compositions.

Hartman, Saidiya V. 1997. *Scenes of Subjection: Terror, Slavery, and Self-making in Nineteenth-Century America*. Oxford: Oxford University Press.

Hartman, Saidiya V., and Frank B. Wilderson III. 2003. "The Position of the Unthought: An Interview." *Qui Parle* 13, no. 2 (spring/summer): 183–201.

Harvey, David. 1993. "From Space to Place and Back Again: Reflections on the Conditions of Postmodernity." In *Mapping the Futures: Local Cultures, Global Change*, ed. Jon Bird, Barry Curtis, Tim Putnam, George Robertson, and Lisa Tickner, 3–29. New York: Routledge.

Haslanger, Sally. 2012. *Resisting Reality: Social Construction and Social Critique*. New York: Oxford University Press.

Hebdige, Dick. 1979. *Subculture: The Meaning of Style*. New York: Routledge.

Helbig, Adriana N. 2014. *Hip Hop Ukraine: Music, Race, and African Migration*. Bloomington: Indiana University Press.

Hendrickson, Hildi, ed. 1996. *Clothing and Difference: Embodied Identities in Colonial and Post-Colonial Africa*. Durham, NC: Duke University Press.

Henry, Paget. 2007. "Africana Political Philosophy and the Crisis of the Postcolony." *Socialism and Democracy* 21, no. 3: 36–59.

Hill Collins, Patricia. 2006. *From Black Power to Hip Hop: Racism, Nationalism, and Feminism.* Philadelphia: Temple University Press.

Hintzen, Percy C., and Jean Muteba Rahier. eds. 2003. *Problematizing Blackness: Self Ethnographies by Black Immigrants to the United States.* New York: Routledge.

Hobson, Janell. 2005. *Venus in the Dark: Blackness and Beauty in Popular Culture.* New York: Routledge.

Hook, Derek. 2008. "The 'Real' of Racializing Embodiment." *Journal of Community and Applied Psychology* 18, no. 2: 140–52.

hooks, bell. 1990. "Postmodern Blackness." *Postmodern Culture* 1, no. 1 (September).

———. 2003. *We Real Cool: Black Men and Masculinity.* New York: Routledge.

Ibrahim, Awad. 2014. *The Rhizome of Blackness: A Critical Ethnography of Hip-Hop Culture, Language, Identity, and the Politics of Becoming.* New York: Peter Lang.

Ignacio, Emily Noelle. 2005. *Building Diaspora: Filipino Cultural Community Formation on the Internet.* New Brunswick, NJ: Rutgers University Press.

Ignatiev, Noel. 1996. *How the Irish Became White.* New York: Routledge.

Instituto das Comunidades. 2007. "Mobilising Cape Verdean Skills Abroad." Praia, Cape Verde.

IOM (International Organization for Migration). 2010. "Cape Verde." https://www.iom.int/cms/en/sites/iom/home.html.

Jackson, John L., Jr. 2001. *Harlemworld: Doing Race and Class in Contemporary Black America.* Chicago: University of Chicago Press.

———. 2005. *Real Black: Adventures in Racial Sincerity.* Chicago: University of Chicago Press.

Jacobson, Matthew Frye. 1999. *Whiteness of a Different Color: European Immigrants and the Alchemy of Race.* Cambridge, MA: Harvard University Press.

James, Robin. 2005. "On Popular Music in Postcolonial Theory." *Philosophia Africana* 8, no. 2 (August): 171–87.

Jones, Rhett. 2003. "Mulattos, Freejacks, Cape Verdeans, Black Seminoles, and Others: Afrocentricism and Mixed-Race Persons." In *Afrocentricity and the Academy: Essays on Theory and Practice*, ed. James L. Conyers Jr., 257–85. Jefferson, NC: McFarland.

Joseph, Ralina L. 2013. *Transcending Blackness: From the New Millennium Mulatta to the Exceptional Multiracial.* Durham, NC: Duke University Press.

Judy, Ronald. 1994. "On the Question of Nigga Authenticity." *Boundary* 21, no. 3: 211–30.

Jung, Moon-Kie, João H. Costa Vargas, and Eduardo Bonilla-Silva. 2011. *State of White Supremacy: Racism, Governance, and the United States.* Palo Alto: Stanford University Press.

Kelley, Robin D. G. 1997. *Yo' Mama's Disfunktional! Fighting the Culture Wars in Urban America.* Boston: Beacon Press.

Kitwana, Bakari. 2014. *Hip-Hop Activism in the Obama Era.* Chicago: Third World Press.

Kolko, Beth E., Lisa Nakamura, and Gilbert B. Rodman, eds. 2000. *Race in Cyberspace.* New York: Routledge.

Levitt, Peggy, and Mary C. Waters, eds. 2002. *Changing Face of Home: The Transnational Lives of the Second Generation.* New York: Russell Sage Foundation.

Lima, Ambrizeth H. 2011. *Cape Verdean Immigrants in America: The Socialization of Young Men in an Urban Environment*. El Paso: LFB Scholarly Publishing.

Lobban, Richard A., Jr. 1995. *Cape Verde: Crioulo Colony to Independent Nation*. Boulder: Westview Press.

Lobban, Richard A., Jr., and Paul Khalil Saucier. 2007. *Historical Dictionary of the Republic of Cape Verde*, 4th ed. Lanham, MD: Scarecrow Press.

Lorick-Wilmot, Yndia S. 2007. "The Role of Social Organizations in Black Ethnic Identity Construction of Post-1965 Caribbean Immigrants in Brooklyn, New York." PhD diss., Northeastern University.

Lott, Eric. 1993. *Love and Theft: Blackface Minstrelsy and the American Working Class*. New York: Oxford University Press.

Lurie, Alison. 2000. *The Language of Clothes*. New York: Owl Books.

Madison, D. Soyini. 2005. *Critical Ethnography: Method, Ethics, and Performance*. Thousand Oaks, CA: Sage.

Mannur, Anita. 2003. "Postscript: Cyberspace and the Interfacing of Diasporas." In *Theorizing Diaspora: A Reader*, ed. Jana Evans Braziel and Anita Mannur, 283–90. Malden, MA: Blackwell.

Martinez, E. 1998. "Beyond Black/White: The Racisms of Our Time." In *The Latino Condition: A Critical Reader*, ed. R. Delgado and Jean Stefancic, 466–77. New York: New York University Press.

Martiniello, Marco. 2002. "Citizenship." In *A Companion to Racial and Ethnic Studies*, ed. David Theo Goldberg and John Solomos, 115–23. Malden, MA: Blackwell.

Massey, Douglas S. 2008. *Categorically Unequal: The American Stratification System*. New York: Russell Sage Foundation.

Massey, Douglas S., and Nancy A. Denton. 1989. "Hypersegregation in U.S. Metropolitan Areas: Black and Hispanic Segregation along Five Dimensions." *Demography* 26:373–91.

Matsuda, Mari. 2002. "Beyond, and Not Beyond, Black and White: Deconstruction Has a Politics." In *Crossroads, Directions, and a New Critical Race Theory*, ed. Francisco Valdes, Jerome McCristal Culp, and Angela P. Harris, 393–398. Philadelphia: Temple University Press.

McClendon, John H. 2005. "Act Your Age and Not Your Color: Blackness as Material Conditions, Presumptive Context, and Social Category." In *White on White/Black on Black*, ed. George Yancy. Lanham, MD: Rowman & Littlefield.

McGahan, Christopher L. 2008. *Racing Cyberculture: Minoritarian Art and Cultural Politics on the Internet*. New York: Routledge.

McKittrick, Katherine. 2011. "On Plantations, Prisons, and a Black Sense of Place." *Social & Cultural Geography* 12, no. 8 (December): 947–63.

McLaren, Peter. 1997. *Revolutionary Multiculturalism: Pedagogies of Dissent for the New Millennium*. Boulder: Westview Press.

Means Coleman, Robin. 2006. "The Gentrification of 'Black' in Black Popular Communication in the New Millennium." *Popular Communication* 4, no. 2: 79–94.

Mehra, Bharat, Cecelia Merkel, and Ann Peterson Bishop. 2004. "The Internet for Empowerment of Minority and Marginalized Users." *New Media & Society* 6, no. 6: 781–802.

Meintel, Deirdre. 1981. *Race, Culture, and Portuguese Colonialism in Cabo Verde*. Syracuse, NY: Syracuse University, Maxwell School of Citizenship and Public Affairs.

Mills, Charles W. 1998. *The Racial Contract*. Ithaca, NY: Cornell University Press.

———. 2013. "An Illuminating Blackness." *The Black Scholar* 43, no. 4 (winter): 32–37.

Monahan, Michael. 2005. "The Conservation of Authenticity: Political Commitment and Racial Reality." *Philosophia Africana* 8, no. 1 (March): 37–50.

Monroe, Barbara. 2004. *Crossing the Digital Divide: Race, Writing, and Technology in the Classroom*. New York: Teachers College Press.

More, Mabogo. 2009. "Black Solidarity: A Philosophical Defense." *Theoria* 56, no. 120 (September): 20–43.

———. 2012. "Black Consciousness Movement's Ontology: The Politics of Being." *Philosophia Africana* 14, no. 1 (March): 23–40.

Moten, Fred. 2003. *In the Break: The Aesthetics of the Black Radical Tradition*. Minneapolis: University of Minnesota Press.

———. 2008. "The Case of Blackness." *Criticism* 50: 177–218.

Mullings, Leith. 2004. "Race and Globalization: Racialization from Below." *Souls* 6, no. 2 (spring): 1–9.

Nakamura, Lisa. 1999. "'Where Do You Want to Go Today?' Cybernetic Tourism, the Internet, and Transnationality." In *Race in Cyberspace*, ed. Beth E. Kolko, Lisa Nakamura, and Gilbert B. Rodman, 15–26. New York and London: Routledge.

———. 2002. *Cybertypes: Race, Ethnicity, and Identity on the Internet*. New York: Routledge.

Nakamura, Lisa, and Peter Chow-White, eds. 2012. *Race after the Internet*. London: Routledge.

Neal, Mark Anthony. 1997. *What the Music Said: Black Popular Music and Black Public Culture*. New York: Routledge.

———. 2001. *Soul Babies: Black Popular Culture and the Post-Soul Aesthetic*. New York: Routledge.

———. 2005. *New Black Man*. New York: Routledge.

———. 2013. *Looking for Leroy: Illegible Black Masculinities*. New York: New York University Press.

Nelson, Alondra, Thuy Linh N. Tu, and Alicia Headlam Hines, eds. 2001. *Technicolor: Race, Technology, and Everyday Life*. New York: New York University Press.

Nopper, Tamara K. 2011. "The Wages of Non-Blackness: Contemporary Immigrant Rights and Discourses of Character, Productivity, and Value." *InTensions* 5 (fall/winter): 1–25.

Ntarangwi, Mwenda. 2009. *East African Hip Hop: Youth Culture and Globalization*. Urbana: University of Illinois Press.

Nyong'o, Tavia. 2009. *The Amalgamation Waltz: Race, Performance, and the Ruses of Memory*. Minneapolis: University of Minnesota Press.

Okpewho, Isidore, and Nkiru Nzegwu. 2009. *The New African Diaspora*. Bloomington: Indiana University Press.

Omi, Michael, and Howard Winant. 1994. *Racial Formation in the United States: From the 1960s to the 1990s*. 2nd ed. New York: Routledge.

Ongiri, Amy Abugo. 2009. *Spectacular Blackness: The Cultural Politics of the Black Power Movement and the Search for a Black Aesthetic*. Charlottesville: University of Virginia Press.

Ortiz, Camilo M. 2012. "Latinos Nowhere in Sight: Erased by Racism, Nativism, the Black-White Binary, and Authoritarianism." *Rutgers Race & the Law Review* 13, no. 2.

Osumare, Halifu. 2013. *The HipLife in Ghana: West African Indigenization of Hip-Hop*. New York: Palgrave-Macmillan.

Pardue, Derek. 2013. "The Role of Creole History and Space in Cape Verdean Migration to Lisbon, Portugal." *Urban Anthropology and Studies of Cultural Systems and World Economic Development* 42, nos. 1 & 2: 95–134.

Perea, Juan F. 1997. "The Black/White Binary Paradigm of Race: The 'Normal Science' of American Racial Thought." *California Law Review* 85, no. 5 (October): 1213–58.

Perry, Imani. 2004. *Prophets of the Hood: Politics and Poetics in Hip Hop.* Durham: Duke University Press.

Pew Internet and American Life Project. 2013. http://pewinternet.org/.

Pierre, Jemima. 2013. *The Predicament of Blackness: Postcolonial Ghana and the Politics of Race.* Chicago: University of Chicago Press.

Pires-Hester, Laura J. 1994. "A Study of Cape-Verdean Ethnic Development: The Emergence of Bilateral Diaspora Ethnicity and Its Impact in a Southeastern New England Locality." PhD diss., Columbia University.

Potter, Russell A. 1995. *Spectacular Vernaculars: Hip-Hop and the Politics of Postmodernism.* Albany: SUNY Press.

"Providence Neighborhood Profiles." www.provplan.org.

Queeley, Andrea. 2003. "Hip-Hop and the Aesthetics of Criminalization." *Souls: A Critical Journal of Black Politics, Culture, and Society* 5, no. 1: 1–15.

Quinn, Eithne. 2004. *Nuthin' but a 'G' Thang: The Culture and Commerce of Gangsta Rap.* New York: Columbia University Press.

Rabaka, Reiland. 2013. *The Hip Hop Movement: From R&B and the Civil Rights Movement to Rap and the Hip Hop Generation.* Lanham, MD: Lexington Books.

Raengo, Alessandra. 2013. *On the Sleeve of the Visual: Race as Face Value.* Hanover, NH: Dartmouth College Press.

Ragnedda, Massimo, and Glenn W. Muschert, eds. 2013. *The Digital Divide: The Internet and Social Inequality in International Perspective.* New York: Routledge.

Rainwater, Lee. 1970. *Behind Ghetto Walls: Black Families in a Federal Slum.* Chicago: Aldine Publishing.

Ramos-Zayas, Ana Y. 2003. *National Performances: The Politics of Class, Race, and Space in Puerto Rican Chicago.* Chicago: University of Chicago Press.

———. 2007. "Becoming American, Becoming Black? Urban Competency, Racialized Spaces, and the Politics of Citizenship among Brazilian and Puerto Rican Youth in Newark." *Identities: Global Studies in Culture and Power* 14: 85–109.

Robinson, Cedric J. 2000. *Black Marxism: The Making of the Black Radical Tradition.* Chapel Hill: University of North Carolina Press.

Rocha, Jorge. 2010. "Genetic Diversity of Cape Verde." *ASemana.*

Rockquemore, Kerry Ann, and David Brunsma. 2008. *Beyond Black: Biracial Identity in America,* 2nd ed. Lanham, MD: Rowman & Littlefield.

Root, Maria P. P., ed. 1992. *Racially Mixed People in America.* Newbury Park, CA: Sage.

———. 1996. *The Multiracial Experience: Racial Borders as the New Frontier.* Thousand Oaks, CA: Sage.

Rose, Tricia. 1994. *Black Noise: Rap Music and Black Culture in Contemporary America.* Middletown, CT: Wesleyan University Press.

———. 2005. "Foreword." In *Black Cultural Traffic: Crossroads in Global Performance and Popular Culture,* ed. Harry J. Elam Jr. and Kennell Jackson, vii–viii. Ann Arbor: University of Michigan Press.

Saldanha, Arun. 2006. "Reontologising Race: The Machinic Geography of Phenotype." *Environment and Planning D: Society and Space* 24, no. 1: 9–24.

———. 2010. "Skin, Affect, Aggregation: Guattarian Variations on Fanon." *Environment and Planning A* 42, no. 10: 2410–27.

Sánchez Gibau, Gina. 1997. "The Politics of Cape Verdean American Identity." *Transforming Anthropology* 6, nos. 1 & 2: 54–71.

———. 2005. "Contested Identities: Narratives of Race and Ethnicity in the Cape Verdean Diaspora." *Identities* 12: 405–38.

Sansone, Livio. 2003. *Blackness without Ethnicity: Constructing Race in Brazil*. New York: Palegrave-Macmillan.

Saucier, P. Khalil, ed. 2011. *Native Tongues: An African Hip-hop Reader*. Trenton, NJ: Africa World Press.

Schloss, Joseph G. 2004. *Making Beats: The Art of Sample-Based Hip-Hop*. Middletown, CT: Wesleyan University Press.

Schulz, David A. 1969. *Coming Up Black: Patterns of Ghetto Socialization*. Englewood Cliffs, NJ: Prentice-Hall.

Sexton, Jared. 2003. "The Consequence of Race Mixture: Racialized Barriers and the Politics of Desire." *Social Identities* 9, no. 2: 241–75.

———. 2008. *Amalgamation Schemes: Antiblackness and the Critique of Multiracialism*. Minneapolis: University of Minnesota Press.

———. 2009. "The Ruse of Engagement: Black Masculinity and the Cinema of Policing." *American Quarterly* 61, no. 1 (March): 39–63.

———. 2010. "People-of-Color-Blindness: Notes on the Afterlife of Slavery." *Social Text*, no. 103 (summer): 31–56.

———. 2011. "The Social Life of Social Death: On Afro-Pessimism and Black Optimism." *InTensions* 5 (fall/winter): 1–47.

Sharma, Nitasha Tamar. 2010. *Hip Hop Desis: South Asian Americans, Blackness, and Global Race Consciousness*. Durham, NC: Duke University Press.

Sharma, Sanjay. 2013. "Black Twitter? Racial Hashtags, Networks and Contagion." *New Formations* 78: 46–64.

Sharpe, Christina. 2010. *Monstrous Intimacies: Making Post-Slavery Subjects*. Durham, NC: Duke University Press.

Sharpley-Whiting, T. Denean. 1999. *Black Venus: Sexualized Savages, Primal Fears, and Primitive Narratives in French*. Durham, NC: Duke University Press.

Shelby, Tommie. 2005. *We Who Are Dark: The Philosophical Foundations of Black Solidarity*. Cambridge, MA: Belknap Press.

Simmel, Georg. 1904. "Fashion." *International Quarterly* 10, no. 1 (October): 130–55, reprinted in *American Journal of Sociology* 62, no. 6 (May 1957): 541–58.

Smith, Andrea. 2010. "Indigeneity, Settler Colonialism, White Supremacy." *Global Dialogue* 12, no. 2 (summer /autumn). http://www.worlddialogue.org/content.php?id=488.

Spillers, Hortense J. 2003. *Black, White, and in Color: Essays on American Literature and Culture*. Chicago: University of Chicago Press.

Stepick, Alex. 1998. *Pride against Prejudice: Haitians in the United States*. Boston: Allyn and Bacon.

Stoller, Paul. 2002. *Money Has No Smell: The Africanization of New York City*. Chicago: University of Chicago Press.

Sundstrom, Ronald R. 2001. "Being and Being Mixed Race." *Social Theory and Practice* 27, no. 2 (April): 285–307.

———. 2008. *The Browning of America and the Evasion of Social Justice*. Albany: SUNY Press.

Telles, Edward E. 2004. *Race in Another America: The Significance of Skin Color in Brazil*. Princeton, NJ: Princeton University Press.

Thomas, Greg. 2007. *The Sexual Demon of Colonial Power: Pan-African Embodiment and Erotic Schemes of Empire*. Bloomington: Indiana University Press.

Thompson, K. 2002. "Border Crossing and Diasporic Identities: Media Use and Leisure Practices of an Ethnic Minority." *Qualitative Sociology* 25, no. 3: 409–18.

Tsing, Anna Lowenhaupt. 2005. *Friction: An Ethnography of Global Connection*. Princeton, NJ: Princeton University Press.

Tulloch, Carol, ed. 2004. *Black Style*. London: Victoria & Albert Museum.

Turner, T. 1980. "The Social Skin." In *Not Work Alone: A Cross-Cultural View of Activities Superfluous to Survival*, ed. Jeremy Cherfas and Roger Lewin, 112–40. London: Temple Smith.

Urdang, Stephanie. 1979. *Fighting Two Colonialisms: Women in Guinea-Bissau*. New York: Monthly Review Press.

U.S. Department of Homeland Security, Office of Immigration Statistics. 2005. *2005 Yearbook of Immigration Statistics*." http://www.dhs.gov/yearbook-immigration-statistics.

U.S. Department of Justice, Immigration and Naturalization Service. 1999. *1999 Statistical Yearbook of the Immigration and Naturalization Service*. https://www.dhs.gov/xlibrary/assets/statistics/yearbook/1999/FY99Yearbook.pdf.

Vale de Almeida, Miguel. 2007. "From Miscegenation to Creole Identity: Portuguese Colonialism, Brazil, Cape Verde." In *Creolization: History, Ethnography, Theory*, ed. Charles Stewart, 108–32. Walnut Creek, CA: Left Coast Press.

Vargas, João H. Costa. 2006. *Catching Hell in the City of Angels: Life and Meanings of Blackness in South Central Los Angeles*. Minneapolis: University of Minnesota Press.

———. 2008. *Never Meant To Survive: Genocide and Utopias in Black Diaspora Communities*. Lanham, MD: Rowman & Littlefield.

———. 2012. "Gendered Antiblackness and the Impossible Brazilian Project: Emerging Critical Black Brazilian Studies." *Cultural Dynamics* 24, no. 1: 3–11.

Vargas, João H. Costa, and Joy A. James. 2012. "Refusing Blackness-as-Victimization: Trayvon Martin and the Black Cyborg." In *Pursuing Trayvon Martin: Historical Contexts and Contemporary Manifestations of Racial Dynamics*, ed. George Yancy and Janine Jones, 193–204. Lanham, MD: Lexington Books.

Wacquant, Loïc. 2007. "French Working-Class Banlieues and Black American Ghetto: From Conflation to Comparison." *Qui Parle* 16, no. 2 (spring/summer): 5–38.

Waters, Mary C. 1994. "Ethnic and Racial Identities of Second-Generation Black Immigrants in New York City." *International Migration Review* 28, no. 4: 795–820.

———. 2001. *Black Identities: West Indian Immigrant Dreams and American Realities*. Cambridge, MA: Harvard University Press.

Watkins, S. Craig. 2005. *Hip Hop Matters: Politics, Pop Culture, and the Struggle for the Soul of a Movement.* Boston: Beacon Press.

Weheliye, Alexander G. 2014. *Habeas Viscus: Racializing Assemblages, Biopolitics, and Black Feminist Theories of the Human.* Durham, NC: Duke University Press.

West, Cornel. 1990. "The New Cultural Politics of Difference." In *Out There: Marginalization and Contemporary Cultures*, ed. Russell Ferguson, Martha Gever, Trinh T. Minh-ha, and Cornel West, 19–38. Cambridge, MA: MIT Press.

Wiegman, Robyn. 1995. *American Anatomies: Theorizing Race and Gender.* Durham, NC: Duke University Press.

Wilderson, Frank B., III. 2009. "Grammar and Ghosts: The Performative Limits of African Freedom." *Theatre Survey* 50, no. 1 (May): 119–25.

———. 2010. *Red, White & Black: Cinema and the Structure of U.S. Antagonisms.* Durham, NC: Duke University Press.

Williams, Raymond. 1977. *Marxism and Literature.* New York: Oxford University Press.

Wilson, Brian. 1996. "It's Gotta Be the Shoes: Youth, Race, and Sneaker Commercials." *Sociology of Sport Journal* 13:398–427.

Woldemikael, Tekle Mariam. 1989. *Becoming Black American: Haitians and American Institutions in Evanston, Illinois.* New York: AMS Press.

Wolfe, Peter. 2002. "Race and Racialization." *Postcolonial Studies* 1, no. 5: 51–62.

Woods, Tryon. 2007. "The Fact of Anti-Blackness: Decolonization in Chiapas and the Niger River Delta." *Human Architecture: Journal of the Sociology of Self-Knowledge* 5, no. 3 (summer): 319–30.

———. 2013. "The Flesh of Amalgamation: Reconsidering the Position (and the Labors) of Blackness." *American Quarterly* 65, no. 2 (June): 437–45.

Wright, Michele M. 2010. "Black in Time: Exploring New Ontologies, New Dimensions, New Epistemologies of the African Diaspora." *Transforming Anthropology* 18, no. 1: 70–73.

Wynter, Sylvia. 2003. "Unsettling the Colonialty of Being/Power/Truth/Freedom: Towards the Human, After Man, Its Overrepresentation—An Argument." *CR: The New Centennial Review* 3, no. 3: 257–337.

Yancy, George. 2005. "'Seeing Blackness' from Within the Manichean Divide." In *White on White/Black on Black*, ed. George Yancy, 233–64. Lanham, MD: Rowman & Littlefield.

Young, Kevin. 2012. *The Grey Album: On the Blackness of Blackness.* Minneapolis: Graywolf Press.

Zack, Naomi. 1993. *Race and Mixed Race.* Philadelphia: Temple University Press.

———, ed. 1995. *American Mixed Race: The Culture of Microdiversity.* Lanham, MD: Rowman & Littlefield.

Žižek, Slavoj. 2005. *Interrogating the Real: Selected Writings.* New York: Continuum.

Index